An Unexpurgated Translation of
BOOK OF SONGS

TRANSLATED, VERSIFIED AND ANNOTATED
BY XU YUANZHONG

Panda Books

Panda Books

First Edition 1994

Copyright 1994 by CHINESE LITERATURE PRESS

ISBN 7−5071−0234−3

ISBN 0−8351−3143−2

Published by CHINESE LITERATURE PRESS

Beijing 100037, China

Distributed by China International Book Trading Corporation

35 Chegongzhuang Xilu, Beijing 100044, China

P.O. Box 399, Beijing, China

Printed in the People's Republic of China

Publisher's Note

The Chinese Literature Press, which published the *Selections from the Book of Songs* in its English Panda Books series ten years ago, is proud to present an unexpurgated English version of the book, translated by Professor Xu Yuanzhong of Peking University.

The *Book of Songs* is the earliest anthology of Chinese poetry. It 305 songs are divided into four parts: "Book of Lyrics (Guofeng)", "Book of Odes (Xiaoya)", "Book of Epics (Daya)", and "Book of Hymns (Song)".

The 160 songs in the "Book of Lyrics" were collected from 15 city states, or fiefs of the Zhou Dynasty. Most of them were created by the working people; the others composed by members of the nobility. All are the cream of China's classical poetry. A number of creative writing techniques had their origin in these songs. These include *fu*, a descriptive rhetorical device with emotional associations, *bi* or smile, a figure of speech in which two unlike things are composed, and *xing* or metaphor, another figure of speech in which a term is transferred from the object it ordinarily designates to an object it may designate only by implicit comparison or analogy. It is with these rhetorical devices and versatile artistic styles that this section of songs gives graphic expression to the ideas, feelings and aspirations of the Chinese who lived more than two thousand years ago.

Most of the odes, epics and hymns in the *Book of Songs* extol the rulers, but there is no lack of poems or lines which poke fun at the evil-doers among these rulers. Some of the compositions throw precious light on life behind the walls of the nobility.

The poems in the *Book of Songs* were composed in what are today's Shaanxi, Shanxi, Hebei, Henan, Shandong and Hubei provinces some 2,500 years ago, and they span a period of five centuries from 1713 BC during the early Zhou Dynasty to 505 BC in the mid-Spring and Autumn Period.

Some historical books, such as *The Historical Records* written by Sima·Qian, claim that the *Book of Songs* was compiled by Confucius.

The *Book of Songs* disappeared when the founding emperor of the Qin Dynasty (221 − 207 BC) launched a campaign in which books were burned and Confucian scholars buried alive. It was not until the Han Dynasty (206 BC − AD 220) that four different compilations of the book were rediscovered. They were *Poetry of Qi* compiled by Yuan Gu of the State of Q*i*, *Poetry of Lu* compiled by Shen Pei of the State of Lu, *Poetry of Han* by Han Ying of the State of Yan, and *Poetry of Mao* by Mao Heng of the State of Lu. After the Eastern Han Dynasty, the *Poetry of Mao* became so popular that the other three versions gradually lost their following until they completely disappeared. The *Book of Songs* which we see today is based on the *Poetry of Mao*.

The *Book of Songs*, whose themes cover a wide cross section of Chinese society, describes the complex social life, the ideas and sentiments of the populace, and the sharpening social conditions in China's remote past. The book is remarkable for its vivid and refined use of a rich vocabulary, life-like characterization and imagery, and soul-touching narration and descriptions. It is, indeed, a glittering gem in the Chinese treasurehouse of literature and history.

CONTENTS

Preface

FEW people in Europe and America know that one of the earliest anthologies of verse in the world is the *Book of Songs* compiled in China 2,500 years ago. This book consists of 305 poems dating from 1713 B.C. (hymn 304 "Rise of the House of Shang") to 505 B. C. (song 133 "Comradeship"). It is divided according to the type of music into four main sections: 160 songs sung by the people in 15 city states and collected by court musicians; 74 odes and 31 epics sung by the nobles at court or at banquets, and 40 hymns used during sacrifice to the gods and ancestors. The section of Hymns is subdivided into "Hymns of Zhou", "Hymns of Lu" and "Hymns of Shang", the last of which is said to be the oldest, dating from between the 17th and the 12th century B. C.

Songs of the early Western Zhou dynasty composed from the 11th to the 9th century B.C. include all the "Hymns of Zhou", a small part of the epics and a few lyrical songs. The majority of these songs are narrative or historical poems, the most outstanding being epic 245 "Hou Ji, the Lord of Corn", epic 250 "Duke Liu", epic 237 "The Migration in 1325 B.C.", epic 241 "Rise of the House of Zhou" and epic 236 "Three Kings of Zhou", all of which describe the founding of the Zhou House. Songs of the later Western Zhou period during the 9th and 8th centuries B.C. include most of the epics and practically all the odes as well as a few folk songs. Some epics and odes extol the military prowess of King Xuan who reigned at the end of the 9th and the beginning of the 8th century B.C. and led expeditions against the frontier tribes. Epic 263 describes his attack on the Xu tribes in the east, in which we find the embryo of Sun Wu's military strategy; ode

177 "General Ji Fu" narrates King Xuan's northern expedition against the Huns and ode 178 "General Fang" his southern campaign against the Chu tribes. These spirited, vigorous yet dignified odes were composed by officials or historians, for example, ode 177 by Zhang Zhong, epic 259 "Count Shen" and epic 260 "Cadet Shan Fu" by General Ji Fu, who is himself glorified in ode 177. Although competent enough, they cannot compare with soldiers' songs like ode 167 "A Homesick Warrior", of which the last stanza was considered the most beautiful verse in the *Book of Songs*.

The best verse comes from Part I: "Book of Lyrics" collected in the Eastern Zhou dynasty from the 8th to the 6th century B.C. Most of the folk songs, written in a simple and natural style, reflect the life and struggle, labor and love, joys and sorrows of the people in ancient times. For instance, song 154 "Life of Peasants" gives a fairly comprehensive picture of the work of the peasants; song 112 "The Woodcutter's Song" satirizes those idle and greedy lords, song 8 sings of the labor of women who gathered plantain seed; song 23 describes a hunter's love, song 1 narrates the life and love of a young man and a fair maiden from spring to winter and their joy at wedding; song 121 expresses the sorrows of peasants, song 29 that of an abandoned woman, song 31 that of a homesick soldier, songs 28 and 17 describe grief at parting and over death.

The "Book of Lyrics" is divided into fifteen sections. The first two sections include eleven songs collected in the south of Zhou and fourteen songs collected south of Zhao, modern Henan. As it is said in the "Great Learning" that the right regulation of the family is the first step toward the good government of all the kingdom, so the folk songs collected south of Zhou and Zhao contain the principles of that regulation, setting forth the virtue of the lord (song 11) and the formalities observed by a woman (wooing and courting in song 1, wedding in song 6, homecoming after the wedding in song 2, married life in song 4, mutual longing after separation in song 3 and child-bearing in song

5). Thus people living south of Zhou and Zhao rejoiced in their domestic happiness and in the number of their children. Purity was seen taking the place of licentiousness, both among women and men. From these songs we can see that regulated families were the basis of a good government in ancient China.

In the second section song 16 celebrates the virtue of the Duke of Zhao, song 15 describes a bride's sacrifice before her wedding, song 12 her arrival at the bridegroom's house, song 24 a princess' wedding, songs 14 and 19 a wife's sorrow at separation with her husband and song 20 the lovesickness of an old maid. Almost all these songs tend to show the importance of married life in a regulated city state.

The third, fourth and fifth sections contain nineteen songs collected in Bei, ten songs collected in Yong and another ten in Wei. When King Wu of Zhou overthrew the Shang Dynasty in 1115 B.C., the domain of its kings was divided by him into three portions, the north of their capital was Bei (modern Hebei), the south was Yong (modern Shandong) and the east was Wei (modern Henan). But long before the time of Confucius, Bei and Yong had been incorporated with the State of Wei, and it was universally acknowledged that the songs of these three sections were all songs of Wei. "As the State of Wei lay along the banks of the Yellow River," said an ancient, "the soil was fertile and did not require much agricultural toil so that the people were indolent. Such was the character of the inhabitants and their songs and music were licentious." Therefore, the licentious Duke Xuan of Wei who took his son's bride as his own in 699 B.C. was censured in song 43, the licentious Duchess Xuan Jiang in song 46 and the licentious people were derided in song 48. But the State of Wei had also many good men. In song 55 appeared Duke Wu who repelled the barbarians' invasion in 770 B.C. and whose equal was hardly to be found in other States; in song 50 appeared Duke Wen, the restorer of the State of Wei. Besides, there were the filial sons of song 32, the faithful official of song 40 and the happy hermit of song 56. All these stood out in a time of degeneracy. Next to them were to be ranked the two brothers of song 44, ready to die for each other. Then there were worthy Duchess Zhuang Jiang of song 28 and patriotic Baroness Mu of Xu of songs 54 and 59. There were, in addition to these heroines, Duchess Dai Wei of song 28, virtuously careful of her person; the wife of song 62, so devoted to her husband; she of song 33, so well acquainted with what constituted virtuous conduct, and she of song 35, cast off and yet maintaining her good name. Thus we see the State of Wei had not only many good men but many wives of ability and virtue.

The sixth section of lyrics collected in the royal domain affords sufficient evidence of the decay of the House of Zhou. It commences with a lamentation over the desolation of the ancient capital and its attached territory where people mourned over the toils of war and the miseries of famine. There are some songs, however which relieve the tension. Song 66 shows us the affection between husband and wife and the pleasantness of their domestic life while song 73 tells us that amid abounding licentiousness the beautiful Lady of Peach Blossom was still faithful to her captive lord and willing to share the same grave with him after their death.

Most songs in the seventh section collected in the State of Zheng (modern Henan) are love songs. Song 89 ''A Lover's Monologue'' shows a woman's longing for her lover; song 85 ''Sing Together'' describes the joy of a songstress dancing with her beloved companion like leaves wafting in the wind; song 90 tells of the delight of a lonely wife on her husband's return on a night of wind and rain; song 76 ''Cadet My Dear'' reveals a young woman's anxiety and fear that her lover might arouse the suspicion of her parents and others. Remarkably in songs of Zheng it is mostly the women who wooed the men and gave expression to their feelings without any appearance of shame or regret, whereas in the love songs of Wei the language is that of the men expressing their feelings of delight in the women. We may find a striking example in song 95 ''Riverside Rendezvous'' in which it is the lass who took the initiative once and again, and song 94 even describes the love-making between a beautiful lass and her lover amid creeping grass overspread with morning dew.

It is strange that in the eighth section of songs collected in Qi (modern Shandong) there is no celebration of the famous Duke Huan but satire against the incest of Duke Xiang with his sister Wen Jiang in songs 101, 102, 104, 105 and 106. Only song 96 ''The Duchess' Admonition'' presents us with a pleasing picture. Songs 97 and 103 show us the vaingloriousness of the officers of the State and their excessive estimation of skill in hunting. Song 100 ''Disorder'' seems to give an indication how ill the court was regulated.

There is no licentious song in the ninth section of songs collected in Wei (modern Shanxi) but satire against idle and greedy lords in songs 112 and 113 and against idle ladies in song 107 and sympathy with poor schloars in songs 108 and 109, with poor soldiers in song 110 and with mulberry gatherers in song 111.

The songs of Tang in the tenth section are those collected in the State of Jin (modern Shanxi), the greatest of the fiefs of Zhou until the rise of Qin (modern Shaanxi). It is also strange that in these songs there is silence about Duke Wen, the hero of the State of Jin, but there is a great deal that is pleasing and has more than a local interest. For instance, song 114 as a picture of cheerful, genial ways of the people, song 121 as an exhibition of filial regard and anxiety and song 124 as a plaintive expression of the feeling of a lonely widow bear to be read and reread. Song 115 ''Why Not Enjoy?'' in the view it gives of death and song 118 in the joy which it describes of a wedding have a human attraction. But there are no such love songs as those of Zheng.

The eleventh section contains songs collected in Qin (modern Shaanxi). Song 126 refers to Lord Zhong who began to turn Qin from a barbarian State to a civilized one in 826 B.C.; songs

127, 128 and 130 to Duke Xiang who defeated the western tribes after they had killed King You in 771 B.C.; song 113 was sung by Duke Ai when he despatched five hundred chariots to the rescue of Chu in 505 B.C. From these songs we can get the idea of Qin as a youthful State, exulting in its growing strength and giving promise of a vigorous manhood. The people rejoiced in their rulers; wives were proud of the martial display of their husbands, while yet they manifested woman's tenderness and affection. Song 131 ''Burial of Three Worthies'' shows what barbarous customs still disfigured Qin's social condition; but there is in the whole an auspice of what the House of Qin became, the destroyer of the effeminated dynasty of Zhou and the establisher of one of its own, based too much on force to be lasting. Many critics think Confucius, the alleged compiler of the *Book of Songs*, gave a place in this collection of songs to those of Qin (Chin) as being prescient of its future history, even the name of China is derived from the Chinese word "Chin" (or "Qin" in normal spelling).

The twelfth section contains ten songs collected in Chen (modern Henan), one of the smaller feudal States of Zhou, with its capital near a mound out of the eastern gate. Its first marchioness was said to be fond of witches and dancers, and so to have affected the manners and customs of the people. Almost all its songs are love songs. Only in songs 138 ''Contentment'', 139 *To a Good Maiden* and 141 ''The Evil-Doer'' have we an approach to correct sentiment and feeling. Song 144 ''The Duke's Mistress'' was said to be the latest of all the songs in the *Book of Songs* to represent Duke Ling as the worst of degeneracy and infamy.

The thirteenth section contains only four songs collected in Gui (modern Henan), a small State misgoverned and extinguished by Duke Wu of Zheng at the time of King Ping's removal to the eastern capital in 769 B.C. In these songs dissoluteness and oppression can be found sapping the foundations of the State; yet there were men painfully conscious of these evils, who saw that the decay of Gui was but a part of the general decay that was at work in the whole kingdom. Of the four songs the third has the greatest merit.

The fourteenth section also contains four songs collected in the small State of Cao (modern Shandong), extinguished by Duke Jing of Song in 487 B.C. Song 151 ''The Poor and the Rich'' shows one of the principal reasons of the decay and ruin of the State, the multiplication of worthless and unprincipled officers. In song 153 ''The Capital'' the writer turned from the misery before his eyes to wistfully recall the glory of bygone days.

The last section contains seven songs collected in Bin (modern Shaanxi), where the first settlers of the House of Zhou had dwelt for nearly five centuries from 1796 to 1325 B.C. Song 154 ''Life of Peasants'' is a valuable record of the manners of an early time with touches of real poetry interpersed. Song 155 ''A Mother Bird'' is the first fable in Chinese poetry. Songs 156, 157 and 159 record the eastern expedition of the Duke of Zhou from 1125 to 1122 B.C. The last song ''An Old Wolf '' gives us an image of the Duke in a dilemma.

As Confucius said, "Poetry may serve to inspire, to reflect, to communicate and to admonish,'' we may say that the ''Book of Lyrics'' serves chiefly to reflect the life of the labouring people, to inspire them to do good and to admonish the rulers against doing wrong. For instance, the first and second sections reflect the domestic life of the ancient Chinese people, the third to fifth sections serve to admonish the lords of their faults, the seventh and twelfth sections are mostly love songs, the thirteenth and fourteenth sections reflect the general decay of the State and the last section inspires the people to admire their Duke.

Part II, ''Book of Odes'', serves chiefly to communicate, to admonish and to reflect the life of the nobles. For instance, the first decade contains six odes used at the royal banquet, the second decade includes two odes used in district entertainment and two describing the royal hunting, the third decade contains an official's complaint against the disorder of the time (ode 181) and a soldier's against the minister of war (ode 185), the fourth decade is composed of complaints against King You and his favorite Lady Shi of Bao (odes 191 − 200), the fifth decade consists of odes of the oppressed nobles and ode 220 ''Revelry'' is a very good picture of the dissipation of the time, the sixth decade is remarkable for odes 211 ''Harvest'' and 212 ''Farm Work'', and the last decade is chiefly censure on King Li's misgovernment. Odes 167 − 169 might be classified as epics for they describe the life of soldiers and generals.

Part III, ''Book of Epics'', records historic deeds and reflects the life of the rulers. For instance, in the first decade there are six epic odes about King Wen, two about King Wu and two about their ancestors King Tai and King Ji (epics 237 and 241). In the second decade epic 245 tells us the story of Hou Ji, Lord of Corn, founder of the Zhou House. There are three epic odes about King Cheng (epics 249, 251, 252) and another three are censures on King Li (epics 253, 254, 255). The first three epic odes in the third decade are admonitions against King Ping (epic 256), King Li (epic 257) and King Xuan (epic 258) respectively, the next three epic odes record the deeds of the Count of Shen (epic 259), Premier Shan Fu (epic 260) and the Marquis of Han (epic 261) and the last two are censures on King You (epics 264, 265).

Part IV, ''Book of Hymns'', serves chiefly to glorify the ancestors of the rulers and inspire their descendents to worship them as gods. The part is divided into three sections: "Hymns of Zhou," "Hymns of Lu" and "Hymns of Shang". In the first decade of the ''Hymns of Zhou'' there are three odes (hymns 266, 267, 268) singing the praises of King Wen, three (hymns 272, 273, 274) of King Wu, four (hymns 269, 270, 271, 274) of King Cheng and one (hymn 275) of Hou Ji, Lord of Corn. The second decade begins with an ode on husbandry (hymn 276) and ends with a hymn to King Wu sung to the music regulating the dance in the temple (hymn 285). Other hymns are sacrificial odes. The third decade is said to be composed by the Duke of Zhou himself as regent. The first seven hymns are all concerned with King Cheng, his ascension in hymn 287, his consultation with his ministers in hymn 288, his self-criticism in hymn 289, his cultivation of the ground in hymn 290 and his thanksgiving sacrifice (hymns 291, 292). The last four hymns (293 – 296) are said to belong to the same series as hymn 285, sung to accompany the dance in honor of King Wu.

The ''Hymns of Lu'' contain only four odes celebrating Duke Xi of Lu, who was in fact a mediocre ruler, but as the descendent of the Duke of Zhou, he was privileged to employ royal ceremonies and sacrifices, which was condemned by Confucius.

The ''Hymns of Shang'' contain five oldest hymns in the Book. Hymn 304 narrates the rise of the House of Shang in 1713 B.C.; hymns 301 – 303 glorify Martial King or King Tang, founder of the Shang dynasty, and the last hymn celebrates his descendent King Wu Ding, who had restored the dynasty to its former glory. Some critics said the ''Hymns of Shang'' were written in the eighth century B.C. by Shang descendents in the State of Song, but there is no authentic proof for it.

Two devices are commonly employed in the *Book of Songs*, the frequent use of simile and metaphor and the practice of starting a poem by employing evocative images quite apart from the central subject. Song 113 is a good example of a poem in which an animal is compared to a certain type of man.

Large rat, large rat,
　Eat no more millet we grow!
Three years you have grown fat.
　No care for us you show.
We'll leave you now, I swear,
　For a happier land,
A happier land where
　In our own place we'll stand.

The longing to go to "a happier land," in other words a society free from tyranny and exploitation, was of course an empty dream at that time; yet it shows the author's rebellious spirit. Sometimes the images first mentioned are related to the general theme like the rat, but again there may be no connection. Certain images have emotional associations; others are chosen solely for the sake of rhyme. For instance, the first stanza of song 112 reads as follows:

> Chop, chop our blows on elm-tree go;
>   On rivershore we pile the wood.
> The clear and rippling waters flow.
> How can those who nor reap nor sow
> Have three hundred sheaves of corn in their place?
> How can those who nor hunt nor chase
> Have in their courtyard badgers of each race?
>   Those lords are good
>   Who do not need work for food!

The first three lines are not closely related to the central subject. Yet this technique of evocative association is widely used in the songs and the odes.

Another striking feature of these poems is the repetition of whole phrases and stanzas, perhaps to show the development of some action, or simply for phonic effect. Occasionally a few words of the first verse are altered to introduce a new rhyme or produce a more melodious effect. The form of repetition varies: sometimes certain stanzas are repeated, sometimes a few lines only, sometimes whole lines and phrases as in song 8.

The metres of Chinese classical poetry may be roughly divided into tetrasyllabic, pentasyllabic and heptasyllabic lines as well as lines of irregular length. The tetrasyllabic lines were the earliest, and most poems in the *Book of Songs* are in this form (e.g. ode 167). Those four-character lines have only two feet each; hence the rhythm is brisk compared with the five and seven-character lines which won popularity later. The great majority of the poems in the *Book of Songs* are rhymed; but the rhyme schemes show a rich variety. Rhymes may be at the end of every line or every alternate line; certain stanzas retain the same rhyme throughout; elsewhere rhymes come in the middle of a line, and sometimes they are reinforced by alliteration. The more than seventy different rhyme patterns in this anthology show how freely rhymes were used.

The vocabulary of the *Book of Songs* is a rich one; so, notably, is the use of epithets, double-adjectives, rhyming words and alliteration, which are used in a variety of ways to heighten the descriptive effect or musical quality of the poems. In addition there are also choruses and refrains, another characteristic feature of folk poetry.

People say that there was no epic in ancient China without knowing the difference between the Chinese epic odes and the Greek epics: the former are historical, emphasizing truth and virtue, while the latter are legendary, emphasizing beauty and violence. For example, we may compare the above-cited ode 236 with a stanza of Pope's translation of Homer's *Iliad*, Book XVI, lines 486−499.

Thestor was next, who saw the chief appear,
And fell the victim of his coward fear;
Shrunk up he sat, with wild and haggard eye,
Nor stood to combat, nor had force to fly:
Patroclus mark'd him as he shunn'd the war,
And with unmanly tremblings shook the car,
And dropp'd the flowing reins. Him 'twixt the jaws,
The javelin sticks, and from the chariot draws.
As on a rock that overhangs the main,
An angler, studious of the line and cane,
Some mighty fish draws panting to the shore:
Not with less ease the barbed javelin bore

> The gaping dastard; as the spear was shook,
> He fell, and life his heartless breast forsook.

This is a meticulously accurate description of the death of Thestor, a Trojan chieftain killed by Patroclus, a Greek chief and Achilles' best friend. The javelin takes away Thestor's dignity as a human being even before it takes his life. He is gaping, like a fish on the hook. The comparison of Patroclus to an angler emphasizes the excitement of the battle. Bernard Knox writes in his introduction to *Masterpieces of the Ancient World*: "Homer's lines here combine two contrary emotions: the human revulsion from the horror of violent death and human attraction to the excitement of the violent action. This passage is typical of the poem as a whole. Everywhere in it we are conscious of these two poles, of war's ugly brutality and its 'terrible beauty.' ... Achilles is a man who lives by and for violence, who is creative and alive only in violent action." In contrast to Homer's or Pope's elaborate and precise description, the Chinese epic odes are simple and concise. Abhorring violence and excess, the Chinese try to secure the mean in their desires and sentiments. Neither violent death nor violent action is described in the *Book of Songs*. The enemy troops defeated and killed are compared to trees cut down, which would bring about no human revulsion; the victorious chief-of-staff is compared to an eagle on the wing, which would arouse no emotional excitement. In a word, we may say that the Homeric epic appeals to passion and the *Book of Songs* to reason.

The Chinese hero looks like Hector, the Trojan hero who fights bravely but reluctantly, whose background is civilized life — the rich city life with its temples and palaces, and continuity of family, and whose preeminence in peace is emphasized by the tenderness of his relation with his wife Andromache. Read for instance the parting scene between them in Homer's *Iliad*, Book VI, lines 624−637:

"Andromache! my soul's far better part,
Why with untimely sorrows heaves thy heart?
No hostile hand can antedate my doom,
'Till fate condemns me to the silent tomb.
Fix'd is the term to all the race of earth;
And such the hard condition of our birth:
No force can then resist, no flight can save,
All sink alike, the fearful and the brave.
No more — but hasten to thy tasks at home,
There guide the spindle, and direct the loom:
Me glory summons to the martial scene,
The field of combat is the sphere for men.
Where heroes war, the foremost place I claim,
The first in danger as the first in fame."

If we compare this farewell speech of Hector's with ode 167, we shall find Homer's description explicit and Hector's sorrow profound, but the description of the Chinese warrior's parting grief implicit and suggestive. The Chinese warrior is reluctant to go to war, but his reluctance is not fully expressed but merely hinted at by the willows' reluctance to part from him. The symbol of willows also shows that there is harmony between man and nature in Chinese poetry while in the Homeric epic we find confrontation and discord between them.

To sum up, Homer, a master at describing strong men and strong feelings, glorifies the heroism of warriors; while the Chinese poets holding to daily life of common people, celebrate the industry of peasants and hunters. The former is romantic and beautiful while the latter is realistic and truthful.

The *Book of Songs* formed an important part of the education of Chinese intellectuals for thousands of years and became one of the classical canons of Confucianism. In this book the ancients learned the way how to regulate a family and how to govern a State, which may be summed up in two words: "rite" and "music." "Rite" imitates the order of the universe;

mitates the harmony of Nature. All things burst forth in spring, grow in summer, mature in autumn and rest in winter, so man should woo in spring, love in summer, be engaged in autumn and wedded in winter in accordance with rite and with the accompaniment of music as shown in song 1. Thus we see rite is instituted to secure the mean in man's desires and music to secure the mean in man's sentiments. Music is benevolence and rite is justice externalized. If a State is governed with rite and music, the people will be just and benevolent and the world will be peaceful and happy. Rite and music are the essence of Confucianism or traditional Chinese culture. In comparison with them, government and law are but secondary. The main function of government and law is but to provide the conditions that make rite and music possible. Educated in Confucianism, China has been standing among the great powers for thousands of years, outshining Egypt and India, Greece and Rome which have only a glorious past, and America and England, France, Germany and Russia which have only a glorious present. From this we can see what an important role the *Book of Songs*, gem of Chinese culture, will play if translated into an English version as beautiful as the original in sense, in sound and in form.

Finally, I would express my grateful acknowledgement to professors Yu Guanying and Jin Qihua for their Chinese vernacular versions of the *Book of Songs* and to Dr. James Legge for the notes he compiled for the *Book of Poetry*.

X.Y.Z.
Peking University
April 18, 1994

Part I

Book of Lyrics

Part I.

Book of Lyrics

(1) SONGS COLLECTED SOUTH OF ZHOU

1. Cooing and Wooing

By riverside are cooing
　A pair of turtledoves;
A good young man is wooing
　A fair maiden he loves.

Water flows left and right
　Of cresses here and there;
The youth yearns day and night
　For the good maiden fair.

His yearning grows so strong,
　He cannot fall asleep;
He tosses all night long,
　So deep in love, so deep!

Now gather left and right
　The cresses sweet and tender!
O lute, play music bright
　For the bride fair and slender!

Feast friends at left and right
　On cresses cooked till tender!
O bells and drums, delight
　The bride so fair and slender!

Note: Turtledoves coo in spring, cresses emerge on water in summer, are gathered in autumn and cooked in winter, so a young man should woo in spring, love in summer, be engaged in autumn and wedded in winter in accordance with the rites and with the accompaniment of music

2. Home-Going

The vines outspread and trail
In the midst of the vale.
Their leaves grow lush and sprout;
Yellow birds fly about
And perch on leafy trees.
O how their twitters please!

The vines outspread and trail
In the midst of the vale.
Their leaves grow lush on soil,
So good to cut and boil
And make cloth coarse or fine.
Who wears it loves the vine.

I tell my mother-in-law
I'll soon homeward go.
I'll wash my undershirt
And rinse my outerskirt.
My dress cleaned, I'll appear
Before my parents dear.

Note: This is a narrative piece in which a married woman tells first of her diligent labor of making cloth of vines and then of her joy of going to pay a
visit of duty and affection to her parents, for home-going was an important
event for a newly-wedded woman after her wedding.

3. A Wife

I gather the mouse-ear
With a basket to fill.
I miss my husband dear
And leave it empty still.

The hill he's climbing up
    May tire his horse, and he
May drink his golden cup
    Lest long he'd think of me.

The height he's climbing up
    May addle his horse on which to roam;
He'd drink his rhino cup
    Lest long he'd think of home.

Climbing the rocky hill,
    His wornout horse can't go;
His servant may be ill.
    O how great is my woe!

Note: The wife is a gatherer of vegetables, unable to fill her basket through the anxiety for the return of her husband, who is absent on some toilsome expedition.

4. Married Happiness

Up crooked Southern trees
    Are climbing creepers' vines;
On lords whom their wives please,
    Quiet happiness shines.

The crooked Southern trees
    Are covered by grapevines;
On lords whom their wives please,
    Greater happiness shines.

Round crooked Southern trees
    Are twining creepers' vines;
On lords whom their wives please,
    Greater happiness shines.

Note: This song celebrates the happiness of married life; the lord is compared to a tree and his wife to the creeper's vine that twines around it.

5. Blessed with Children

Insects in flight,
  Well you appear.
It is all right
  You've many children dear.

Insects in flight,
  How sound your wings!
It is all right
  You've children in long strings.

Insects in flight,
  You feel so warm.
It is all right
  Your children come in swarms.

Note: This song offers blessing to those who have children by comparing them to insects that cluster together in harmony and consequently increase at a wonderful rate.

6. The Newly-Wed

The peach tree beams so red,
  How brilliant are its flowers!
The maiden's getting wed,
  Good for the nuptial bowers.

The peach tree beams so red,
  How plentiful its fruit!

The maiden's getting wed;
    She's the family's root.

The peach tree beams so red,
    Its leaves are lush and green.
The maiden's getting wed;
    On household she'll be keen.

Note: Under the Zhou dynasty all the young people were married in the middle of spring when the peach tree was in flower. Here the bride's beauty and fertility and the household's prosperity are compared to peach flower, fruit and leaves.

7. Warriors

Well set are rabbit nets;
    On the pegs go the blows.
The warriors our lord gets
    Protect him from the foes.

Well set are rabbit nets,
    Placed where crossroads appear.
The warriors our lord gets
    Will be his good compeer.

Well set are rabbit nets,
    Amid the forest spread.
The warriors our lord gets
    Serve him with heart and head.

Note: This is a praise of the warriors raised from such a low position as a rabbit-catcher to such a high position as the lord's compeer, if they would serve him heart and soul.

8. Plantain Gathering

We gather plantain seed.
Let's gather it with speed!
We gather plantain ears.
Let's gather them with cheers!

We gather plantain seed.
Let's rub it out with speed!
We gather plantain ears.
Pull by handfuls with cheers!

We gather plantain seed.
Let's fill our skirts with speed!
We gather plantain ears.
Belt up full skirts with cheers!

Note: This was a song sung at work by women gathering plantain seeds
which were thought to be favorable to child-bearing.

9. A Woodcutter's Love

I find no welcome shade
    In branchless southern tree;
I cannot reach the maid
    Roaming the river free.
The river is so wide,
I cannot reach the other side;
The river is so long,
I cannot cross its current strong.

I'd cut with all my force
    The thorns beneath the tree;

I would fain feed her horse
  If she should marry me.
The river is so wide,
I cannot reach the other side;
The river is so long,
I cannot cross its current strong.

I would cut all the weeds
  And thorns beneath the tree;
I'd feed her pony-steeds
  If she should marry me.
The river is so wide,
I cannot reach the other side;
The river is so long,
I cannot cross its current strong.

Note: A woodcutter expresses his love for a maiden living on the other side
of the river which he could not cross.

10. A Wife Waiting

Along the raised bank green
  I cut down twigs and wait.
My lord cannot be seen;
  I feel a hunger great.

Along the raised bank green
  I cut fresh sprigs and sprays.
My lord can now be seen;
  I feel not cast away.

The bream has fire-red tail;
  Like fire the orders press.
They press to what avail?

Our parents in distress.

Note: The wife cuts down twigs on the bank to see whether her lord is coming home, and she feels a great sexual hunger on not seeing him. Just home, he is to leave again, pressed by royal orders, and his wife tries to persuade him to stay under the pretext that their parents would be distressed by his departure. According to some commentator, the wife tries to dissuade her lord from leaving her again by cooking for him a red-tailed fish so as to show the unfed flame of her heart.

11. The Good Unicorn

The unicorn will use its hoofs to tread on none
Just like our prince's noble son.
Ah! they are one.

The unicorn will knock its head against none
Just like our prince's grandson.
Ah! they are one.

The unicorn will fight with its horn against none
Just like our prince's great-grandson.
Ah! they are one.

Note: The unicorn is a fabulous animal, the symbol of all goodness and benevolence, having the body of a deer, the tail of an ox, the hoofs of a horse, one corn, the scales of a fish, etc. Its hoofs are here mentioned because it does not tread on any living thing, not even on live grass; its head because it does not butt with it; and its horn because the end of it is covered with flesh, to show that the creature, while able for war, wills to have peace. This poem celebrates the goodness of the offspring of King Wen (1184-1134 BC), founder of the Zhou dynasty (1121-225 BC).

(2) SONGS COLLECTED SOUTH OF ZHAO

12. The Bride

The magpie builds a nest,
　　Where comes the dove in spring.
The bride comes fully-dressed,
　　Welcomed by cabs in a string.

The magpie builds a nest,
　　Where dwells the dove in spring.
The bride comes fully-dressed,
　　Escorted by cabs in a string.

The magpie builds a nest,
　　Where lives the dove in spring.
The bride comes fully-dressed,
　　Adored by cabs in a string.

Note: This song celebrates the marriage of a bride (compared to a dove or cuckoo or myna) to a lord (compared to a magpie) and the splendor of the nuptials.

13. The Sacrifice

Gather southernwood white
　　By the pools here and there.
Employ it in the rite
　　In our prince's affair.

Gather southernwood white
　　In the vale by the stream.
Employ it in the rite

Under the temple's beam.

Wearing black glossy hair,
　　We're busy all the day.
With dishevelled hair
　　At dusk we go away.

Note: This song narrates the industry and reverence of a prince's chamber-maids, assisting the prince in sacrificing.

14. Absence

Hear grassland insects sing
And see grasshoppers spring!
When my lord is not seen,
I feel a sorrow keen.
When I see him downhill
And meet him by the rill,
My heart will then be still.

I go up southern hill;
Of ferns I get my fill.
When my lord is not seen,
I feel a grief more keen.
When I see him downhill
And meet him by the rill,
My heart with joy will thrill.

I go up southern hill;
Of herbs I get my fill.
When my lord is not seen,
I feel a grief most keen.
When I see him downhill
And meet him by the rill,

My heart will be serene.

Note: The wife of a lord bewails his absence on duty and longs for his return from autumn when grasshoppers sing, to spring when fern is gathered, and to summer when herb is gathered.

15. Sacrificial Offerings

Where to gather duckweed?
  In the brook by south hill.
Where to gather pondweed?
  Between the brook and rill.

Where to put what we've found?
In baskets square or round.
Where to boil what we can?
In tripod or a pan.

Where to put offerings?
In the temple's both wings.
Who offers sacrifice?
The bride-to-be so nice.

Note: Daughters should be trained in the business of sacrifices for three months previous to their marriage. This song tells us how offerings are gathered and boiled in the ancestral temple.

16. The Duke of Zhao

O leafy tree of pear!
Don't clip or make it bare,
For once our Duke lodged there.

O leafy tree of pear!
Don't break its branches bare,
For once our Duke rested there.

O leafy tree of pear!
Don't bend its branches bare,
*For once our Duke halted there.

Note: The Duke of Zhao was a principal adherent of King Wen (1184-1134
BC). The love of the people for the memory of the Duke of Zhao makes
them love the trees beneath which he had rested.

17. I Accuse

The path with dew is wet;
Before dawn off I set;
I fear no dew nor threat.

Who says in sparrow's head
    No beak can pierce the roof?
Who says the man's not wed?
    He jails me without proof.
He can't wed me in jail;
I'm jailed to no avail.

Who says in the rat's head
    No teeth can pierce the wall?
Who says the man's not wed?
    He brings me to judge's hall.
    Though brought to judge's hall,
    I will not yield at all.

Note: A young woman resists the attempt to force her to marry a married
man and, though put in jail and brought to the judge's hall, she still argues
her case.

18. Officials

In lamb and sheep skins dressed,
  With their five braidings white,
They come from court to rest,
  And swagger with delight.

In sheep and lamb skins dressed,
  With five seams of silk white,
They swagger, come to rest,
  And take meals with delight.

In lamb and sheep furs drest,
  with their five joinings white,
They take their meals and rest,
  And swagger with delight.

Note: It is said that this song is a satire on those officials who only delight in taking meals and resting and do nothing else of consequence.

19. Return

The thunder rolls away
  O'er southern mountain's crest.
Why far from home do you stay,
  Not daring take a rest?
My lord for whom I yearn,
  Return! return!

The thunder rolls away
  By southern mountain's side.
Why far from home do you stay,
  Not daring take a ride?

My lord for whom I yearn,
    Return! return!

The thunder rolls away
    At southern mountain's foot.
Why far from home do you stay
    As if you'd taken root?
My lord for whom I yearn,
    Return! return!

Note: A young wife, on hearing the thunder, is led to think of her husband
who is absent on public service.

20. An Old Maid

The fruits from mume-trees fall,
    One-third of them away.
If you love me at all,
    Woo me a lucky day!

The fruits from mume-trees fall,
    Two-thirds of them away.
If you love me at all,
    Woo me this very day!

The fruits from mume-trees fall,
    Now all of them away.
If you love me at all,
    You need not woo but say.

Note: According to ancient custom, young people should get married in
spring. When mume fruit falls, it is summer and maidens over twenty might
get married without courtship.

21. A Concubine

The starlets shed weak light,
    Three or five o'er east gate.
Having passed with my lord the night,
    I hurry back lest I'd be late:
    Such is a concubine's fate.

The starlets shed weak light,
    With the Pleiades o'erhead.
Having passed with my lord the night,
    I hurry back with sheets of bed.
    What else can I do instead?

Note: A concubine is returning from a visit to her lord's bedchamber at
early dawn for only the wife could pass the whole night with her husband
while a concubine was admitted only for a short time and must go and return in the dark; hence the tradition of comparing a concubine to a starlet.
According to some commentators, this song is the complaint of a petty official who should get up by starlight and go to bed by starlight.

22. A Deserted Wife

Upstream go you
To wed the new
And leave the old.
You leave the old:
Regret foretold.

Downstream go you
To wed the new
And forsake me.
You forsake me;
Rueful you'll be.

Bystream go you
To wed the new
And desert me.
You desert me;
Woeful you'll be.

Note: A merchant's wife complains that she is left, forsaken and deserted by
her husband, and she foretells that he will be rueful and woeful, which
shows that she still cherishes the wish for reconciliation or retaliation.

23. A Deer-killer and a Jadelike Maiden

An antelope is killed
And wrapped in white afield.
A maid for love does long,
Tempted by hunter strong.

He cuts down trees amain
And kills a deer again.
He sees the white-dressed maid
As beautiful as jade.

"Oh, soft and slow, sweetheart!
Don't tear my sash apart!"
The jadelike maid says, "Hark!
Do not let the dog bark!"

Note: This song hints at the love-making between a hunter and a beautiful
maiden. The fresh openness of feeling here harmonizes with the sense of
spring in the countryside.

24. The Princess's Wedding

Luxuriant in spring
    As plum flowers o'er water,
How we revere the string
    Of cabs for the king's daughter!

Luxuriant in spring
    As the peach flowers red,
The daughter of the king
    To a marquis' son is wed.

We use the silken thread
    To form a fishing line.
The son of a marquis is wed
    To the princess divine.

Note: This song describes the marriage of the granddaughter of King Ping (769-719 BC) and the son of the Marquis of Qi. The silken thread forming a fishing line may allude to the newly-wed forming a happy family.

25. A Hunter

Abundant rushes grow along;
One arrow hits one boar among.
Ah! What a hunter strong!

Abundant reeds along the shores,
One arrow scares five boars.
Ah! What a hunter one adores!

Note: This song sings the praise of a huntsman of the prince's park.

(3) SONGS COLLECTED IN BEI

26. Complaint of a Woman

Like cypress boat
Mid-stream afloat,
I cannot sleep
In sorrow deep.
I won't drink wine,
Nor roam nor pine.

Unlike the brass
Where images pass,
On brothers I
Cannot rely.
When I complain,
I meet disdain.

Have I not grown
Firm as a stone?
Am I as flat
As level mat?
My mind is strong:
I've done no wrong.

I'm full of spleen,
Hated by the mean;
I'm in distress,
Insulted no less;
Thinking at rest,
I beat my breast.

The sun and moon
Turn dim so soon.

I'm in distress
Like a dirty dress.
Silent think I:
Why can't I fly?

Note: We have in this song the complaint of a woman neglected by her husband, disdained by her brothers and envied and hated by his mean concubines. Some commentator who interprets this song as complaint of a man says that it was the forerunner of *Sorrow after Departure*, a poem written by Qu Yuan (340-278 BC).

27. My Old Mate

The upper robe is green;
　　Yellow the lower dress.
My sorrow is so keen;
　　When will end my distress?

The upper robe is green;
　　Yellow the dress with dots.
My sorrow is so keen;
　　How can it be forgot?

The silk is green that you,
　　Old mate, dyed all night long;
I miss you, old mate, who
　　Kept me from doing wrong.

The linen coarse or fine
　　Is cold when blows the breeze.
I miss old mate of mine,
　　Who put my mind at ease.

Note: A widower misses his deceased wife who made his green robe and yellow dress for him. This was the first elegy in Chinese poetry.

28. A Farewell Song

A pair of swallows fly
With their wings low and high.
You go home in your car;
I see you off afar.
When your car disappears,
Like rain fall down my tears.

A pair of swallows fly;
You go home with a sigh.
When they fly up and down,
I see you leave the town.
When your car disappears,
I stand there long, in tears.

A pair of swallows fly,
Their songs heard far and nigh.
You go to your home state;
I see you leave the south gate.
When your car disappears,
Deeply grieved I shed tears.

My faithful sister dear
With feeling e'er sincere,
So gentle and so sweet,
So prudent and discreet!
The thought of our late lord
Strikes our sensitive chord.

Note: This is the first farewell song in Chinese literature. Lady Zhuang Jiang relates her grief at the departure of Lady Dai Wei who was obliged to return to her native State of Chen when her son, Duke Huan of Wei, brought up by Lady Zhuang Jiang, was murdered by her half-brother Zhou Yu in 718 BC.

29. An Abandoned Woman

Sun and moon bright,
   Shed light on earth!
This man in sight
   Without true worth
Has set his mind
To be unkind.

Sun and moon bright
   Cast shade with glee.
This man in sight
   Would frown at me.
He's set his mind
To leave me behind.

Sun and moon bright
   Rise from the east.
This man in sight
   Is worse than beast.
His mind is free
To forget me.

Sun and moon bright
   From east appear.
Can I requite
   My parents dear?
My mind not set,
Can I forget?

Note: It is said that the abandoned woman refers to Lady Zhuang Jiang
who complains of and appeals against the bad treatment she received from
Zhou Yu, who murdered in 718 BC his half-brother, Duke Huan of Wei,
brought up by Lady Zhuang Jiang, and usurped the dukedom.

30. Yearning

The wind blows violently;
He looks and smiles at me.
With me he seems to flirt;
My heart feels deeply hurt.

The wind blows dustily;
He's kind to come to me.
Should he nor come nor go,
How would my yearning grow!

The wind blows all the day;
The clouds won't fly away.
Awake, I'm ill at ease.
Would he miss me and sneeze!

In gloomy cloudy sky
The thunder rumbles high.
I cannot sleep again.
O would he know my pain!

Note: This is the description of a feminine mind after a man's flirtation with her. It is also said to be the complaint of Lady Zhuang Jiang who bemoaned the supercilious treatment she received from her frivolous lord.

31. Complaint of Warriors

The drums are booming out;
We leap and bound about.
Some build walls high and low;
Others should southward go.

We follow Sun Zi-zhong
To fight with Chen and Song.
We cannot homeward go;
Our hearts are full of woe.

Where stop and stay our forces
When we have lost our horses?
Where can we find them, please?
They're found among the trees.

We parted, live or die;
We made oath, you and I.
When can our hands we hold
And live till we grow old?

Alas! so long we've parted.
Can I live broken-hearted?
Alas! the oath we swore
Can be fulfilled no more.

Note: soldiers of Wei lament their separation from their families after the war
on Chen in 718 BC.

32. Our Mother

From the south blows the breeze
Amid the jujube trees.
The trees grow on the soil;
We live on mother's toil.

From the south blows the breeze
On branches of the trees.
Our mother's good to sons;
We are not worthy ones.

The fountain's water runs
  To feed the stream and soil.
Our mother's seven sons
  Are fed by her hard toil.

The yellow birds can sing
  To comfort us with art.
We seven sons can't bring
  Comfort to mother's heart.

Note: Seven sons of some family in Wei blame themselves for the
unhappiness of their mother in her state of widowhood.

33. My Man in Service

The male pheasant in flight
Wings its way left and right.
O dear one of my heart!
We are so far apart.

See the male pheasant fly;
Hear his song low and high.
My man is so sincere.
Can I not miss him so dear?

Gazing at moon or sun;
I think of my dear one.
The way's a thousand *li*.
How can he come to me?

But if he's really good,
He will do what he should.
For nothing would he long.
Will he do anything wrong?

Note: A wife deplores the absence of her husband and celebrates his virtue.

34. Waiting for Her Fiance

The gourd has leaves which fade;
The stream is deep to wade.
　If shallow, leap!
　And strip if deep!

See the stream's water rise;
Hear female pheasant's cries.
The stream wets not the axle straight;
The pheasant's calling for her mate.

Hear the song of wild geese;
　See the sun rise in glee.
Come before the streams freeze
　If you will marry me.

I see the boatman row
　Across but I will wait;
With others I won't go:
　I will wait for my mate.

Note: A woman is waiting for her fiance by the riverside on an autumn morning when the leaves of the gourd are fading and the water is rising with the rising sun.

35. A Rejected Wife

Gently blows eastern breeze
　With rain 'neath cloudy skies.
Let's set our mind to please
　And let no anger rise!

Who gathers plants to eat
    Should keep the root in view.
Do not forget what's meet
    And me who'd die with you!

Slowly I go my way;
    My heart feels sad and cold.
You go as far to say
    Goodbye as the threshold.
Is lettuce bitter? Nay,
    To me it seems e'en sweet.
Feasting on wedding day,
    You look as brothers meet.

The by-stream is not clear,
    Still we can see its bed.
Feasting your new wife dear,
    You treat the old as dead.
Do not approach my dam,
    Nor move my net away!
Rejected as I am,
    What more have I to say?

When the river was deep,
    I crossed by raft or boat;
When 'twas shallow, I'd keep
    Myself aswim or afloat.
I would have spared no breath
    To get what we did need;
Wherever I saw death,
    I would help with all speed.

You loved me not as mate;
    Instead you gave me hell.
My virtue caused your hate

As wares which did not sell.
In days of poverty
    Together we shared woe;
Now in prosperity,
    I seem your poison slow.

I've vegetables dried
    Against the winter cold.
Feast them with your new bride
    Not your former wife old.
You beat and scolded me
    And gave me only pain.
The past is gone, I see,
    And no love will remain.

Note: This is the plaint of a wife rejected and supplanted by another to whom she speaks in lines 5-6 of stanza 3. In stanza 4 the wife sets forth how diligent and thoughtful she had been in her domestic affairs; in stanza 5 she dwells on her husband's hostile feeling to her in his prosperity; in stanza 6 she says still she will return good for evil.

36. Toilers

It's near dusk, lo!
Why not home go?
It is for you
We're wet with dew.

It's near dusk, lo!
Why not home go?
For you, O Sire,
We toil in mire.

Note: This is the toilers' complaint against the Marquis of Wei.

37. Refugee

The high mound's vines appear
   So long and wide.
O cousin dear,
   Why not come to my side?

Why dwell you thereamong
   For other friends you make?
Why stay so long?
   For who else's sake?

Furs in a mess appear;
   Eastward goes not your cart.
O cousin dear,
   Don't you feel sad at heart?

So poor and base appear
   The refugee.
O cousin dear,
   Why don't you listen to me?

Note: This is a complaint of a deserted woman, or of the refugees in Wei
against those who did not assist them. In stanza 1 they refer to the length of
the vines to show how long they had been waiting in vain; in stanza 2 they
seem to account for their dilatoriness; in stanza 3 they advance to the charge
of want of sympathy; in stanza 4 their piteous condition is described.

38. A Dancer

With main and might
   Dances the ace.
Sun at its height,

He holds his place.

He dances long
   With might and main;
Like tiger strong
   He holds the rein.

A flute in his left hand,
   In his right a plume fine,
Red-faced, he holds command,
   Given a cup of wine.

Hazel above,
   Sweet grass below.
Who is not sick for love
   Of the Dancing Beau?
Who is not sick for love
   Of the Western Beau?

Note: Stanza 1 describes the dancer or the Dancing Beau; stanza 2 his military dance; stanza 3 his civil dance; in the last stanza the Western Beau is said to refer to the Marquis of Wei who rewarded the dancer with a cup of wine.

39. Homesickness

The bubbling water flows
   From the spring to the stream.
My heart to homeland goes;
   Day and night I seek dreams.
I'll ask my cousins dear
How I may start from here.

I will lodge in one place,
   Take my meal in another,

And try to find the trace
  How I parted from mother.
I'll ask about aunts dear
On my way far from here.

I'll lodge in a third place
  And dine in a fourth one.
I'll set my cab apace;
  With axles greased 'twill run.
I'll hasten to go home.
Why should I not have come?

When I think of Fair Spring,
  How can I not heave sighs!
Thoughts of my homeland bring
  Copious tears to my eyes.
I drive to find relief
And drown my homesick grief.

Note: Baroness Mu of Xu, a daughter of the House of Wei, married in the
State of Xu, expresses her longing to revisit Wei (Fair Spring).

40. A Petty Official

Out of north gate
  Sadly I go.
I'm poor by fate.
  Who knows my woe?
  Let it be so!
Heaven wills this way.
What can I say?

I am busy about
  Affairs of royalty.

When I come from without,
  I'm blamed by family.
  So let it be!
Heaven wills this way.
What can I say?

I am busier about
  Public affairs, but oh!
When I come from without,
  I'm given blow on blow.
  Let it be so!
Heaven wills this way.
What can I say?

Note: A petty officer of Wei sets forth his hard lot and his silence under it in submission to Heaven. The object of the song, it is said, is to expose the government of Wei, which neglected men of such worth.

41. The Hard Pressed

The cold north wind does blow,
And thick does fall the snow.
  To all my friends I say:
"Hand in hand let us go!
  There's no time for delay;
  We must hasten on our way."

The sharp north wind does blow,
And heavy falls the snow.
  To all my friends I say:
"Hand in hand far away let's go!
  There's no time for delay;
  We must hasten on our way."

Red-handed foxes glow,
With their hearts black as crows.
　To all my friends I say:
"In my cart let us go!
　There's no time for delay;
We must hasten on our way."

Note: Some lord of Wei presses his friends to leave the country with him at
once in consequence of the prevailing oppression and misery. The first two
lines in all the stanzas are a metaphorical description of the miserable condition of the State. Fox and crow were both creatures of evil omen.

42. A Mute Maiden

A maiden mute and tall
Trysts me at corner wall.
I can find her nowhere
And scratch my head in despair.

The maiden fair and mute
Gives me a grass-made lute.
Playing a rosy air,
I'm happier than e'er.

Coming back from the mead,
She gives me a rare reed,
Lovely not for it's rare:
It's given by the fair.

Note: The three stanzas describe the three trysts between a young man and
a young shepherdess. The shepherdess does not appear in the first tryst and
gives her lover a grass-made lute in the second and a rare reed in the third.
This is the first song in Chinese poetry in which the poet shows his participa-
tion in the feeling of things.

43. Complaint of a Duchess

How bright is the new tower
   On brimming river deep!
Of youth she seeks the flower,
   Not loathsome toad to keep.

How high is the new tower
   On flowing river deep!
Of youth she seeks the flower,
   Not stinking toad to keep.

A net for fish is set;
   A toad is caught instead.
The flower of youth she'll get,
   Not a hunchback to wed.

Note: This is a satire against Duke Xuan of Wei who took his son's bride as his own wife and built a new tower by the Yellow River to welcome her in 699 BC. The toad refers to the duke and the flower to his son.

44. My Two Sons

My two sons take a boat;
Downstream their shadows float.
I miss them when they're out;
My heart is tossed about.

My two sons take a boat;
Far, far away they float.
I think of them so long.
Would no one do them wrong!

Note: Duke Xuan of Wei who had taken his eldest son's bride as his own plotted to get rid of this son by sinking his boat, but his younger son, aware of this design, insisted on going in the same boat with his elder brother, and their mother, worried, wrote this song.

45. A Determined Woman

A cypress boat
Midstream afloat.
Two tufts of hair o'er his forehead,
He is my mate to whom I'll wed.
I swear I will not change my mind till dead.
Heaven and mother,
Why don't you understand another?

A cypress boat
By riverside afloat.
Two tufts of hair o'er his forehead,
He is my only mate to whom I'll wed.
I swear I will not change my mind though dead.
Heaven and mother,
Why don't you understand another?

Note: This song of a determined woman was mistaken for that of a chaste widow.

46. Scandals

The creepers on the wall
    Cannot be swept away.
Stories of inner hall
    Should not be told by day.
What would have to be told
Are scandals manifold.

The creepers on the wall
    Cannot be rooted out.
Scandals of inner hall

Should not be talked about.
If they are talked of long,
They'll be an endless song.

The creepers on the wall
  Cannot be together bound.
Scandals of inner hall
  Should not be spread around.
If spread from place to place,
They are shame and disgrace.

Note: The things done in the harem of the palace of Wei were too shameful
to be told. Duke Xuan was notorious for his licentiousness. His first wife
was a lady of his father's harem, called Yi Jiang, by an incestuous connection with whom he had a son called Ji Zi, who became his heir-apparent.
By and by he contracted a marriage for his son with Xuan Jiang; but on her
arrival in Wei, moved by her youth and beauty, he took her himself (See'
song 43) and by her he had two sons, Shou and Shuo. Yi Jiang hanged herself in vexation and the duke was prevailed on, in course of time, by the in-
trigues of Xuan Jiang and Shuo, to consent to the death of Ji Zi, Shou per-
ishing in a noble but fruitless attempt to preserve his life (it was said the two
sons in song 44 refer to Ji Zi and Shou). In the next year the duke died
and was succeeded by Shuo.

47. A Lady

She'd live with her lord till old,
Adorned with gems and gold.
Stately and full of grace,
Stream-like, she goes her pace.
As a mountain she'll dwell;
Her robe becomes her well.
A lady to adore,
What needs her lord for more?

She is so bright and fair

In pheasant-figured gown.
Like a cloud is her black hair,
    No false locks but her own.
Her earrings are of jade,
Her pin of ivory made.
Her forehead's white and high,
Like a goddess from the sky.

She is so fair and bright
In rich attire snow-white.
O'er her fine undershirt
She wears a close-fitting skirt.
Her eyes are bright and clear;
    Her face will fascinate.
How can she not appear
    A beauty of the state!

Note: The lady refers to Xuan Jiang (See Note to song 46) and her lord to
Zhao Bo, son of Duke Xuan of Wei and father of Baroness Mu of Xu (See
song 54). This is one of the two earliest poems describing the beauty of a
lady in Chinese literature.

48. Trysts

"Where gather golden thread?"
    "In the fields over there."
"Of whom do you think ahead?"
    "Jiang's eldest daughter fair."
She did wait for me 'neath mulberry,
In upper bower tryst with me
And see me off on the River Qi.

"Where gather golden wheat?"
    "In northern fields o'er there."
"Whom do you long to meet?"

"Yi's eldest daughter fair."
She did wait for me 'neath mulberry,
In upper bower tryst with me
And see me off on the River Qi.

"Where gather mustard plant?"
  "In eastern fields o'er there."
"Who does your heart enchant?"
  "Yong's eldest daughter fair."
She did wait for me 'neath mulberry,
In upper bower tryst with me
And see me off on the River Qi.

Note: This is one of the earliest love songs in Chinese literature. It was said to be directed against the licentiousness which prevailed in Wei, for a new daughter comes up in every stanza.

49. Misfortune

The quails together fly;
  The magpies sort in pairs.
She takes an unkind guy
  For brother unawares.

The magpies sort in pairs;
  The quails together fly.
For master unawares
  She takes an unkind guy.

Note: Duchess Xuan Jiang in song 47 was first raped by Duke Xuan of Wei (master) and then by his son Zhao Bo (brother). She was not so fortunate as quails and magpies which have a faithful mate.

50. Duke Wen of Wei

At dusk the four stars form a square;
   It's time to build a palace new.
The sun and shade determine where
   To build the palace at Chu,
To plant hazel and chestnut trees,
   Fir, yew, plane, cypress. When cut down,
Some are used to make lutes to please
   The ducal crown.

The duke ascends the ruined wall
   To view the site of the capital
And where to build his palace hall.
He then surveys the mountain's height
   And comes down to see mulberries.
The fortune-teller says it's right
   And the duke is pleased with all of these.

After the fall of vernal rain
   The duke orders his groom to drive
His horse and cab with might and main.
   At mulberry fields they arrive;
To farmers he is good indeed:
   He wishes husbandry to thrive
And three thousand horses to breed.

Note: After the death of the last duke of Wei in 659 BC, Duke Wen moved
the capital to Cao and built a new palace at Chu. As he was diligent and
sympathetic with the people, the State of Wei became prosperous under his
reign.

51. Elopement

A rainbow rises in the east;
  To point to it nobody dares.
A maid eloping like a beast
  Will leave her parents in despair.

The morning clouds rise in the west,
  Foretelling rain all the day.
A maid eloping is not blest;
  Her parents will weep far away.

A maid eloping like this one
  Won't wed according to the rite.
She is obedient to none
  And leaves her parents in sad plight.

Note: This is a song against lewd connections. A rainbow is regarded as the result of an improper connection between the light and the dark, the masculine and feminine principles of nature, and so it is an emblem of improper connections between men and women. The superstition prevails of holding it unlucky to point to a rainbow in the east: an ulcer will forthwith be produced in the offending hand. The meaning of the first stanza is that as the rainbow in the east is not fit to be pointed to, so the elopement is not fit to be spoken about.

52. The Rat

The rat has skin, you see?
Man must have decency.
If he lacks decency,
Worse than death it would be.

The rat has teeth, you see?

Man must have dignity.
If he lacks dignity,
For what but death waits he?

The rat has limbs, you see?
Man must have propriety.
Without propriety,
It's better dead to be.

Note: A man without decency, dignity and propriety is not equal to a rat.

53. Betrothal Gifts

The flags with ox-tail tied
Flutter in countryside.
Adorned with silk bands white,
Four steeds trot left and right.
What won't I give and share
With such a maiden fair?

The falcon-banners fly
In the outskirts nearby.
Adorned with ribbons white,
Five steeds trot left and right.
What won't I give and send
To such a good fair friend?

The feathered streamers go down
All the way to the town.
Bearing rolls of silk white,
Six steeds trot left and right.
What and how should I say
To her as fair as May?

Note: The procession carrying betrothal gifts appears first in the countryside, then in the outskirts and finally by the town-walls. In the last two lines of each stanza the speaker expresses his admiration of his fiancee.

54. Patriotic Baroness Mu of Xu

I gallop while I go
To share my brother's woe.
I ride down a long road
To my brother's abode.
The deputies will thwart
My plan and fret my heart.

"Although you say me nay,
I won't go back the other way.
Conservative are you
While farsighted is my view.
Although you say me nay,
I won't stop on my way.
Conservative are you,
I can't accept your view."

I climb the sloping mound
To pick toad-lilies round.
Of woman don't make light!
My heart knows what is right.
My countrymen put blame
On me and feel no shame.

I go across the plains;
Thick and green grow the grains.
I'll plead to mighty land.
Who'd hold out helping hand?

"Deputies, don't you see
The fault lies not with me?
Whatever your design,
It's not so good as mine."

Note: This is the first poem written by a poetess in Chinese literature. Baroness Mu of Xu, daughter of Duchess Xuan Jiang (See song 47), complains of not being allowed to go to Wei, to condole with her brother Duke Wen on the desolation of his State after the death of Duke Dai in 659 BC. Her plan was to appeal to some great power. As it was contrary to the rules of propriety for a lady in her position to return to her native State, the deputies of Wei did not allow her to do so.

(5) SONGS COLLECTED IN WEI

55. The Duke of Wei

Behold by riverside
  Green bamboos in high glee.
Our duke is dignified
  Like polished ivory
And stone or jade refined.
  With solemn gravity
And elevated mind,
  The duke we love a lot
  Should never be forgot.

Behold by riverside
  Bamboos with soft green shade.
Our duke is dignified
  When crowned with strings of jade
As bright as stars we find.
  With solemn gravity
And elevated mind,
  The duke we love a lot
  Should never be forgot.

Behold by riverside
  Bamboos so lush and green.
Our duke is dignified
  With gold- or tin-like sheen.
With his sceptre in hand,
  He is in gentle mood;
By his chariot he'd stand;
  At jesting he is good,
  But he is never rude.

Note: This is a poem in praise of Duke Wu who ruled the State of Wei in 811-757 BC. The Duke cultivated the principles of government, the people increased in number and others flocked to the State. In 770 BC when King You of Zhou was killed by a barbarian tribe, the Duke led a body of soldiers to the assistance of Zhou and did great service against the enemy, so that King Ping appointed him a minister of the court.

56. A Happy Hermit

By riverside unknown
  A hermit builds his cot.
He sleeps, wakes, speaks alone:
  Such joy won't be forgot.

By mountainside unknown
  A hermit will not fret.
He sleeps, wakes, sings alone:
  A joy ne'er to forget.

On wooded land unknown
  A hermit lives, behold!
He sleeps, wakes, dwells alone:
  A joy ne'er to be told.

Note: This is the first poem in praise of a hermit's life in Chinese literature. It was said that this song was directed against Duke Zhuang, who did not walk in the footsteps of his father Wu, and by his neglect of his duties led men of worth to withdraw from public life into retirement.

57. The Duke's Bride

The buxom lady's big and tall,
  A cape o'er her robe of brocade.
Her father, brothers, husband all

Are dukes or marquis of high grade.

Like lard congealed her skin is tender,
    Her fingers like soft blades of reed;
Like larva white her neck is slender,
    Her teeth like rows of melon-seed.
Her forehead like a dragonfly's,
    Her arched brows curved like a bow.
Ah! dark on white her speaking eyes,
    Her cheeks with smiles and dimples glow.

The buxom lady goes along;
    She passes outskirts to be wed.
Four steeds run vigorous and strong,
    Their bits adorned with trappings red.
Her cab with pheasant-feathered screen
    Proceeds to the court in array.
Retire, officials, from the scene!
    Leave duke and her without delay!

The Yellow River wide and deep
    Rolls northward its jubilant way.
When nets are played out, fishes leap
    And splash and throw on reeds much spray.
Richly-dressed maids and warriors keep
    Attendance on her bridal day.

Note: The Duke's bride refers to the beautiful Lady Zhuang Jiang who was
married to Duke Zhuang of Wei but bore no children and brought up Duke
Huan who was murdered by his half-brother Zhou Yu in 718 BC (See song
28). Stanza 1 describes her arrival in Wei and her great connections; stanza
2 is occupied with her personal beauty, the earliest description of its kind in
Chinese poetry; stanza 3 describes her appearance and equipage as she
draws near to the capital of Wei; stanza 4 may hint at love-making, with the
fish symbolic of the duke and water symbolic of his bride.

58. A Faithless Man

A man seemed free from guile;
In trade he wore a smile.
He'd barter cloth for thread;
No, to me he'd be wed.
I saw him cross the ford,
But gave him not my word.
I said by hillside green,
"You have no go-between.
Try to find one, I pray.
In autumn be the day."

I climbed the wall to wait
To see him pass the gate.
I did not see him pass;
My tears streamed down, alas!
When I saw him pass by,
I'd laugh with joy and cry.
Both reed and tortoise shell
Foretold all would be well.
"Come with your cart," I said,
"To you I will be wed."

How fresh were mulberries
With their fruit on the trees!
Beware, O turtledove,
Eat not the fruit of love!
It will intoxicate.
Do not repent too late!
Man may do what he will,
He can atone it still.
No one will e'er condone
The wrong a woman's done.

The mulberries appear
With yellow leaves and sear.
E' er since he married me,
I' ve shared his poverty.
Deserted, from him I part;
The flood has wet my cart.
I have done nothing wrong;
He changes all along.
He' s fickle to excess,
Capricious, pitiless.

Three years I was his wife
And led a toilsome life.
Each day I early rose
And late I sought repose.
But he found fault with me
And treated me cruelly.
My brothers who didn' t know
Let their jeers at me go.
Mutely I ruminate
And I deplore my fate.

I' d live with him till old;
My grief was not foretold.
The endless stream has shores;
My endless grief e' er pours.
When we were girl and boy,
We' d talk and laugh with joy.
He pledged to me his troth.
Could he forget his oath?
He' s forgot what he swore.
Should I say any more?

Note: This is the first long song in the " Book of Lyrics " . A cast-off woman relates and bemoans her sad case. In stanza 3, the turtledove drunk with mul-

berries represents the woman who had been indiscreet. In stanza 4 the woman returns to her original home; in stanza 5 her brothers ignorant of all the circumstances will not acknowledge her, her parents supposed to be dead. The last line may be expanded into the following: What then can be done? It is all over; yes, all over.

59. A Lovesick Fisherman

With long rod of bamboo
    I fish in River Qi.
Dear, how I think of you,
    Far-off a hundred *li*!

At left the Spring flows on;
    At right the River clear.
To wed they saw you gone,
    Leaving your parents dear.

The River clear at right,
    At left the Spring flows on.
O your smiles beaming bright
    And ringing gems are gone!

The long, long River flows
    With boats of pine home-bound.
My boat along it goes.
    O let my grief be drowned!

Note: A fisherman is longing for his love married far beyond the River Qi, whose shores were lovers' rendezvous in the third lunar month. By "fishing" we may understand "love-making" in the *Book of Songs*. The first stanza may imply that, long as my fishing rod is, I cannot reach my love married a hundred *li* away.

60. A Conceited Youth

The creeper's pods hang like
A young man's girdle spike.
An adult's spike he wears;
For us he no longer cares.
He puts on airs and swings
To and fro his tassel-strings.

The creeper's leaves also swing;
The youth wears an archer's ring.
An archer's ring he wears;
For us he no longer cares.
He puts on airs and swings
To and fro his tassel-strings.

Note: It was said that the subject of this song is Duke Hui of Wei, Shuo,
the son of Xuan and Xuan Jiang, who succeeded to the State after the murder of his brothers, Ji Zi and Shou (See Note to song 46). He was then
young, 15 or 16. The creeper in line 1 is weak, unable to rise from the
ground without support; it is introduced here with an allusion to the weak
character of the youth who is spoken of. The spike in line 2 is worn at the
girdle for the purpose of loosening knots; it belongs to the equipment of grown-
up men, and is supposed to indicate their competency for the management
of business, however intricate. The youth in the song assumes it from vani-
ty. The ring in the 2nd stanza is worn by archers on the thumb of the right
hand to assist them in drawing the string of their bow; the verse is
condemnatory of the youth pretending to be a man but without a man's
knowledge or ability.

61. Homeland

Who says the River's wide?
A reed can reach the other side.
Who says my home is far-off? Lo!
I can see it on tiptoe.

Who says the River 's wide?
A boat can cross the tide.
Who says my home is far away?
I can reach it within a day.

Note: A daughter of Xuan Jiang was married to Duke Huan of Song on the
other side of the Yellow River. After giving birth to a son, who became
Duke Xiang, she was divorced and returned to Wei. When that son succeeded to Song, she wished to return to that State; but the rules of propriety forbade her, as having been divorced, to do so; and she is supposed
to have made these verses to reconcile herself to her circumstances. They are
supposed, therefore, to be much to her honor, as showing how she could
subordinate her maternal longings to her sense of what was proper.

62. My Lord

My lord is brave and bright,
    A hero in our land,
A vanguard in the King's fight,
    With a lance in his hand.

Since my lord eastward went,
    Like thistle looks my hair.
Have I no anointment?
    For whom should I look fair?

Let it rain, let it rain!
    The sun shines bright instead.
I miss my lord in vain,
    Heedless of my aching head.

Where's the Herb to Forget?
    To plant it north I'd start.
Missing my lord, I fret:

It makes me sick at heart.

Note: A wife mourns over the protracted absence of her husband on the king's service in the year 706 BC when Duke Xuan of Wei did service with the king. This was considered as the earliest song of a wife longing for her husband in service.

63. A Lonely Husband

Like lonely fox he goes
    On the bridge over there.
My heart sad and drear grows:
    He has no underwear.

Like lonely fox he goes
    At the ford over there.
My heart sad and drear grows:
    He has no belt to wear.

Like lonely fox he goes
    By riverside o'er there.
My heart sad and drear grows:
    He has no clothes whate'er.

Note: A woman expresses her longing for her husband who is lonely, far from home, in misery and desolation.

64. Gifts

She throws a quince to me;
    I give her a green jade
Not in return, you see,
    But to show acquaintance made.

She throws a peach to me;
  I give her a white jade
Not in return, you see,
  But to show friendship made.

She throws a plum to me;
  I give her jasper fair
Not in return, you see,
  But to show love for e'er.

Note: This love song refers to the interchange of courtesies between a lover and his mistress. Small gifts of kindness should be responded to with greater gratitude, for friendship is more than any gift.

(6) Songs Collected Around the Capital

65. The Ruined Capital

The millet drops its head;
　The sorghum is in sprout.
Slowly I trudge and tread;
　My heart is tossed about.
Those who know me will say
　My heart is sad and bleak;
Those who don't know me may
　Ask me for what I seek.
O boundless azure sky,
Who's ruined the land and why?

The millet drops its head;
　The sorghum in the ear.
Slowly I trudge and tread;
　My heart seems drunk and drear.
Those who know me will say
　My heart is sad and bleak;
Those who don't know me may
　Ask me for what I seek.
O boundless azure sky,
Who's ruined the land and why?

The millet drops its head;
　The sorghum is in grain.
Slowly I trudge and tread;
　My heart seems choked with pain.
Those who know me will say
　My heart is sad and bleak;
Those who don't know me may
　Ask me for what I seek.
O boundless azure sky,

Who's ruined the land and why?

Note: In 769 BC King Ping of the Zhou dynasty removed the capital to the east and from that time the kings of Zhou sank nearly to the level of the princes of the States. An official seeing the desolation of the old capital wrote this song expressing his melancholy and grief.

66. My Man is Away

My man's away to serve the state;
I can't anticipate
How long he will there stay
Or when he'll be on homeward way.
The sun is setting in the west;
The fowls are roosting in their nest;
The sheep and cattle come to rest.
To serve the state my man's away.
How can I not think of him night and day?

My man's away to serve the state;
I can't anticipate
When we'll again have met.
The sun's already set;
The fowls are roosting in their nest;
The sheep and cattle come to rest.
To serve the state my man's away.
Keep him from hunger and thirst, I pray.

Note: This is the forerunner of frontier poetry. It expresses the feeling of a wife on the prolonged absence of her husband on service and her longing for his return.

67. What Joy

My man sings with delight;
   In his left hand a flute of reed,
He calls me to sing with his right.
   What joy indeed!

My man dances in delight;
   In his left hand a feather-screen,
He calls me to dance with his right.
   What joy foreseen!

Note: This song is regarded as a sequel of the preceding one, expressing the
wife's joy on her husband's return.

68. In Garrison

Slowly the water flows;
   Firewood can't be carried away.
To my wife my thought goes:
   In garrison she cannot come and stay.
How much for her I yearn!
O when may I return?

Slowly the water flows;
   No thorn can be carried away.
To my wife my thought goes:
   In army camp she cannot come and stay.
How much for her I yearn!
O when may I return?

Slowly the water flows;
   Rushes can't be carried away.

To my wife my thought goes:
　　In army tent she cannot come and stay.
How much for her I yearn!
O when may I return?

Note: The troops of Zhou, kept on duty in the State of Shen, murmur at their separation from their families. The water which flows so slowly and whose power is so weak that it cannot carry away firewood or thorn or rushes may allude to the Kingdom of Zhou, too weak to defend its frontiers.

69. Regret

Amid the vale grow mother-worts;
　　They are now withered and dry.
There's a woman her lord deserts.
　　O hear her sigh!
　　O hear her sigh!
Her lord's a faithless guy.

Amid the vale grow mother-worts;
　　They are now scorched and dry.
There's a woman her lord deserts.
　　O hear her cry!
　　O hear her cry!
She has met a bad guy.

Amid the vale grow mother-worts;
　　They are now drowned and wet.
There's a woman her lord deserts.
　　See her tears jet!
　　See her tears jet!
It's too late to regret.

Note: This song is expressive of pity for the suffering wife, deserted by her husband like the withered mother-worts, now scorched in the sun, now drowned in water.

70. Past and Present

The rabbit runs away,
   The pheasant is in the net.
In my earliest days
   For nothing did I fret;
In later years of care
   All evils have I met.
O I would sleep fore'er.

The rabbit runs away,
   The pheasant is in the snare.
In my earliest days,
   For nothing did I care;
In later years of ache
   I'm in grief and despair.
I'd sleep and never wake.

The rabbit runs away,
   The pheasant is in the trap.
In my earliest days
   I lived without mishap;
But in my later years
All miseries appear.
I'd sleep and never hear.

Note: An officer of Zhou declares his weariness of life because of the growing miseries of the State. The rabbit is said to be of a secret and crafty nature while the pheasant is bold and determined. The former, consequently, is snared with difficulty while the latter is easily taken. In the rabbit we have the mean men who stirred up disorder and then contrived to escape from its consequences; in the pheasant, the superior men who would do their duty in times of trouble and suffered.

71. Strangers

Creepers spread all the way
  Along the river clear.
From brothers far away,
  I call a stranger "father dear".
Though called " dear father", he
Seems not to care for me.

Creepers spread all the way
  Beside the river clear.
From brothers far away,
  I call a stranger "mother dear".
Though called "dear mother", she
Seems not to cherish me.

Creepers spread all the way
  Beyond the river clear.
From brothers far away,
  I call a stranger "brother dear".
Though called "dear brother", he
Seems not to pity me.

Note: A wanderer from Zhou, separated from his kin, mourns over his lot.
The thick, continuous growth of the creepers on the soil proper to them is
presented by the speaker in contrast to his own position, torn from his family and proper soil.

72. One Day When I See Her Not

To gather vine goes she.
When her I do not see,
One day seems longer than months three.

To gather reed goes she.
When her I do not see,
One day seems long as seasons three.

To gather herbs goes she.
When her I do not see,
One day seems longer than years three.

Note: The speaker longs for the society of a maiden who gathers vine, reed and herbs. A short absence from her seems to be long, and longer the more it is dwelt upon.

73. I Miss You

Rumbling your cart,
  Reedlike your gown,
I miss you in my heart.
  How dare I make it known?

Rattling your cart,
  Reddish your gown,
I miss you in my heart.
  How dare I have it shown?

Living, we dwell apart;
  Dead, the same grave we'll share.
Am I not true at heart?
  By the bright sun I swear.

Note: The beautiful Lady of Peach Blossom missed her lord, a captive of the prince of Chu. "Rumbling" and "rattling" denote the noise made by the cart of the prince, carrying criminals to prison. In the last stanza the lady gives expression to her attachment: the lovers might be kept apart all their lives, but they would be united in death and lie in the same grave. In the last two lines she says, "These are words from my heart. If you think that my words are not sincere, there is a Power above like the bright sun observing me. How should my words not be sincere?''

74. To A Lover

I wait for you on the hemp mound,
But I don't see you come around.
When I see you come round,
How happy I'll be found!

I wait for you among the wheat,
But I don't see you on your feet.
When I see you on your feet,
I'll give you fruit to eat.

I wait for you beneath plum tree,
But I don't see you come with glee.
When I see you in glee,
You'll give your girdle gems to me.

Note: A woman longs for the presence of her lover and the last line may hint at love-making, for he is supposed to give her his girdle gems after love is made.

(7) SONGS COLLECTED IN ZHENG

75. A Good Wife

The black-dyed robe befits you well;
    When it's worn out, I'll make another new.
You go to work in your hotel;
    Come back, I'll make a meal for you.

The black-dyed robe becomes you well;
    When it's worn out, I'll get another new.
You go to work in your hotel;
    Come back, I'll make a meal for you.

The black-dyed robe does suit you well;
    When it's worn out, you'll have another new.
You go to work in your hotel;
    Come back, I'll make a meal for you.

Note: It is said that this song is expressive of the wife's regard that was due
to the virtue and ability of her lord.

76. Cadet My Dear

    Cadet my dear,
Don't leap into my hamlet, please,
Nor break my willow-trees!
Not that I care for these;
It is my parents that I fear.
Much as I love you, dear,
How can I not be afraid
Of what my parents might have said!

Cadet my dear,
Don't leap over my wall, please,
Nor break my mulberries!
Not that I care for these;
It is my brothers that I fear.
Much as I love you, dear,
How can I not be afraid
Of what my brothers might have said!

Cadet my dear,
Don't leap into my garden, please,
Nor break my sandal trees!
Not that I care for these;
It is my neighbors that I fear.
Much as I love you, dear,
How can I not be afraid
Of what my neighbors might have said!

Note: A woman begs her lover to let her alone, and not arouse the suspicions of her parents and others.

77. The Young Cadet

The young cadet to chase has gone;
It seems there's no man in the town.
Is it true there's none in the town?
It's only that I cannot find
Another hunter so handsome and kind.

The young cadet has gone hunting in the wood;
In the town there's no drinker good.
Is it true there's no drinker good?
In the town no drinker of wine
Looks so handsome and fine.

The young cadet has gone to the countryside;
In the town there's none who can ride.
Is it true there's none who can ride?
I cannot find among the young and old
Another rider so handsome and bold.

Note: The young cadet is said to refer to Duan, younger brother of Duke
Zhuang of Zheng who succeeded Duke Wu in 742 BC, and to whom his
mother had a great dislike while Duan was her favorite. At the mother's
solicitation, Duan was invested with a large city and he proceeded, in con-
cert with her, to form a scheme for wresting the dukedom from Duke
Zhuang. The issue was the ruin of Duan.

78. Hunting

Our lord goes hunting in the land,
   Mounted in his cab with four steeds.
He waves and weaves the reins in hand;
   Two outside horses dance with speed.
Our lord goes hunting in the grass lands;
   The hunters' torches flame in a ring.
He seizes a tiger with bare hand
   And then presents it to the king.
Don't try, my lord, to do it again
For fear you may get hurt with pain.

Mounted in his chariot and four,
   Hunting afield our lord does go.
Two inside horses run before;
   Two on the outside follow in a row.
Our lord goes to the waterside;
   The hunters' torches blaze up high.
He knows not only how to ride
   But also shoots with his sharp eye.
He runs and stops his steeds at will

And shoots his arrows with great skill.

Mounted in cab and four steeds fine,
　Our lord goes hunting in the lands.
Two on the inside have their heads in a line;
　Two on the outside follow like two hands.
To waterside our lord does go;
　The hunters' fire spreads everywhere.
His grey and yellow steeds go slow;
　The arrows he shoots become rare.
Aside his quiver now he lays
And returns his bow to the case.

Note: This song celebrates the charioteering and archery of Duan, younger
brother of Duke Zhuang of Zheng. This is the earliest description of hunting
in Chinese poetry.

79. Qing Warriors

Qing warriors stationed out,
Four mailed steeds run about.
Two spears adorned with feathers red,
Along the stream they roam ahead.

Qing warriors stationed on the shore
Look martial in their cab and four.
Two spears with pheasant's feathers red,
Along the stream they stroll ahead.

Qing warriors stationed on the stream
Look proud in their cab and mailed team.
Driver at left, spearsman at right,
The general shows his great delight.

Note: This is a satire against Duke Wen who ruled in Zheng (662-627 BC) but manoeuvred uselessly an army of Qing on the frontiers.

80. Officer in Lamb's Fur

His fur of lamb is white
As the man is upright.
The officer arises
Unchanged in a crisis.

With cuffs of leopard-skin,
The fur of lamb he's in
Makes him look strong and bold;
To the right he will hold.

His fur of lamb is bright
With three stripes left and right.
The officer stands straight,
A hero of the state.

Note: This song celebrates some officer of Zheng for his elegant appearance and integrity. He wore at audiences the upper garment made of lamb's skin, distinguished by cuffs or ornaments of leopard-skin. This song is ironical because there was no such officer in Zheng.

81. Leave Me Not

I hold you by the sleeve
    Along the public way.
O do not hate and leave
    A mate of olden day!

I hold you by the hand

Along the public road.
Don't think me ugly and
Leave your former abode!

Note: A woman entreats her lover not to leave their abode along the public road and cast her off.

82. Domestic Life

The wife says, "Cocks crow, hark!"
The man says, "It's still dark."
"Rise and see if it's night;
The morning star shines bright."
"Wild geese and ducks will fly;
I'll shoot them down from high."

"At shooting you are good;
I'll dress the game as food.
Together we'll drink wine
And live to ninety-nine.
With zither by our side,
In peace we shall abide."

"I know your wifely care;
I'll give you pearls to wear.
I know you will obey;
Can pearls and jade repay?
I know your steadfast love;
I value nothing above."

Note: This is a pleasant picture of domestic life. In stanza 1 the wife sends her husband from her side to his hunting; in stanza 2 she expresses her affection for him and in stanza 3 he expresses his for her.

83. Lady Jiang

A lady in the cab with me
Looks like a flower from a hedge-tree
She goes about as if in flight,
Her girdle-pendants look so bright.
O Lady Jiang with pretty face,
So elegant and full of grace!

The lady together with me
Walks like a blossoming hedge-tree.
She moves about as if in flight;
Her girdle-pendants tinkle light.
O Lady Jiang with pretty face,
Can I forget you so full of grace?

Note: It is said that this is spoken by a lover about his mistress Lady Jiang, but the language is that of respect more than of love.

84. A Joke

Uphill stands a mulberry
    And a lotus in the pool.
The handsome one I do not see;
    Instead I see a fool.

Uphill stands a pine-tree
    And in the pool are leaves of red.
The pretty one I do not see;
    I see the sly one instead.

Note: A woman mocks her lover as a sly fool, saying that the hill and the pool are furnished with what is most natural and proper to them, but it is not so with her and her friend.

85. Sing Together

Leaves sear, leaves sear,
   The wind blows you away.
Sing, cousins dear,
   And I'll join in your lay.

Leaves sear, leaves sear,
   The wind wafts you away.
Sing, cousins dear,
   And I'll complete your lay.

Note: When leaves waft in the wind after harvest, a songstress asks her companions to sing and dance together like the wafting leaves.

86. A Handsome Guy

You handsome guy
   Won't speak to me words sweet.
For you I sigh
   And can neither drink nor eat.

You handsome guy
   Won't eat with me at my request.
For you I sigh
   And cannot take my rest.

Note: A woman complains of her handsome lover.

87. To a Seeming Lover

If you think of me as you seem,
Lift up your robe and cross that stream!
If you don't love me as you seem,

Can I not find another one?
Your foolishness is second to none.

If you think of me as you seem,
Lift up your gown and cross this stream!
If you don't love me as you seem,
Can I not find a better mate?
Your foolishness is really great.

Note: A woman sings to her seeming lover who would not lift up his robe
and cross the stream to meet her.

88. Lost Opportunity

You looked plump and plain
And waited for me in the lane.
Why did I not go with you? I complain.

You looked strong and tall
And waited for me in the hall.
I regret I did not return your call.

Over my broidered skirt
I put on simple shirt.
O Sir, I say:
Come in your cab and let us drive away!

I put on simple shirt
Over my broidered skirt.
O Sir, I say anew:
Come in your cab and take me home with you!

Note: A woman regrets that she did not meet the advances of one who
sought her love and wishes that he would come again.

89. A Lover's Monologue

"At eastern gate on level ground
There are madder plants around.
My lover's house is very near,
But far away he does appear.

"'Neath chestnut tree at eastern gate
Within my house in vain I wait.
How can I not think of my dear?
Why won't he come to see me here?"

Note: A woman thinks of her lover's residence and complains that he does
not come to her. The eastern gate was that of the capital of Zheng, the principal gate of the city. There was an open space about it, which may explain
the reference to the "level ground." Near this was a bank where the
madder plant was cultivated. On the space also was a road, along which
chestnut trees were planted, and by one or more of them was a row of
houses. In this row lived the object of the woman's affection. The house
was near, but the man was distant; not really so, but as she did not see
him, it was the same to her, as if he were far away.

90. Wind and Rain

The wind and rain are chill;
The crow of cocks is shrill.
When I've seen my man best,
Should I not feel at rest?

The wind whistles with showers;
The cocks crow dreary hours.
When I've seen my dear one,
With my ill could I not have done?

Gloomy wind and rain blend;

The cocks crow without end.
When I have seen my dear,
How full I feel of cheer!

Note: This describes the joy of a lonely wife on seeing her husband return
on a night of wind and rain.

91. To a Scholar

Student with collar blue,
How much I long for you!
Though to see you I am not free,
O why don't you send word to me?

Scholar with belt-stone blue,
How long I think of you!
Though to see you I am not free,
O why don't you come to see me?

I'm pacing up and down
On the wall of the town.
When to see you I am not free,
One day seems like three months to me.

Note: A woman mourns the indifference and absence of her lover, a student
wearing blue gems at the girdle and a blue collar, designation for a graduate
of the first degree.

92. Believe Me

Wood bound together may
Not be carried away.
We have but brethren few;
There're only I and you.

What others say can't be believed,
Or you will be deceived.

A bundle of wood may
Not be carried away.
We have but brethren few;
There are only we two.
Do not believe what others say!
Untrustworthy are they.

Note: A woman asserts good faith to her husband and protests against people who would sow doubt and jealousy between them. A bundle of firewood may allude to a couple well united.

93. My Lover in White

Outside the eastern gate
Like clouds fair maidens date.
Though they are fair as clouds,
My love's not in the crowd.
Dressed in light green and white,
Alone she's my delight.

Outside the outer gate
Like blooms fair maidens date.
Though like blooms they're fair,
The one I love's not there.
Dressed in scarlet and white,
She alone gives me delight.

Note: A man praises his lover dressed in light green or scarlet and white, contrasted with beautiful maidens dating outside the eastern gate of the capital of Zheng.

94. A Beautiful Lass

Afield the creeping grass
  With crystal dew o'erspread,
There's a beautiful lass
  With clear eyes and fine forehead.
When I meet the clear-eyed,
My desire's satisfied.

Afield the creeping grass
  With round dewdrops o'erspread,
There's a beautiful lass
  With clear eyes and fine forehead.
When I meet the clear-eyed,
Amid the grass let's hide!

Note: This song describes the love-making of a young man and a beautiful lass amid the creeping grass fresh with morning dew.

95. Riverside Rendezvous

The Rivers Zhen and Wei
Overflow on their way.
The lovely lad and lass
Hold in hand fragrant grass.
"Let's look around," says she;
"I have already," says he.
  "Let us go there again!
Beyond the River Wei
The ground is large and people gay."
  Playing together then,
They have a happy hour;
Each gives the other a peony flower.

The Rivers Zhen and Wei
  Flow crystal-clear;
Lad and lass squeeze their way
  Through the crowd full of cheer.
"Let's look around," says she;
"I have already," says he.
  "Let us go there again!
Beyond the River Wei
The ground is large and people gay."
  Playing together then,
They have a happy hour;
Each gives the other a peony flower.

Note: It was the custom of the State of Zheng for young men and women to meet and make love by the riverside on the festive day of the third lunar month in spring.

(8) SONGS COLLECTED IN QI

96. The Duchess' Admonition

"Wake up!" she says, "Cocks crow.
The court is on the go."
"It's not the cock that cries,"
He says, "but humming flies."

"The east is brightening;
The court is in full swing."
"It's not the east that's bright
But the moon shedding light."

"See buzzing insects fly.
It's sweet in bed to lie.
But courtiers will not wait;
None likes you to be late."

Note: A model duchess urges her husband to rise early and attend to his duties. The first two lines of stanzas 1 and 2 are to be taken as the language of the good wife, thinking it was time for her husband to be stirring and give audience in his court. Lines 3 and 4 are taken as the reply of the duke to the call to him to get up, indicative of his habits of luxurious self-indulgence and indolence. Stanza 3 is to be taken as the language of the wife, coaxing the duke to get up. Line 3 speaks of the ministers or officers assembled in the court. If the duke did not soon appear, they would return to their own houses or offices. The last line means: "Do not let them, on my account, make you also the object of their dislike."

97. Two Hunters

How agile you appear!
    Amid the hills we meet.
Pursuing two boars, compeer,
    You bow and say I'm fleet.

How skilful you appear!
We meet halfway uphill.
Driving after two males, compeer,
You bow and praise my skill.

How artful you appear!
South of the hill we meet.
Pursuing two wolves, compeer,
You bow and say my art's complete.

Note: This song is referred to the Duke of Qi (934-894 BC), like the last,
and is said to be directed against his inordinate love of hunting, which in-
fected the manners of the officers and people. In the first line of each stanza,
the speaker praises another; in the last, that other praises him; in the third,
he takes credit to himself and the other for ability. The poet simply relates
his words without any addition of his own, it is a specimen of admirable satire through which the boastful manners of the people of Qi are clearly exhib-
ited.

98. The Bridegroom

He waits for me between the door and screen,
His crown adorned with ribbons green
Ended with gems of beautiful sheen.

He waits for me in the court with delight,
His crown adorned with ribbons white
Ended with gems and rubies bright.

He waits for me in the inner hall,
His crown adorned with yellow ribbons all
Ended with gems like golden balls.

Note: A bride describes her first meeting with the bridegroom who should
wait for her arrival first at the door, then in the court and at last in the inner
hall, according to ancient nuptial ceremony.

99. Nocturnal Tryst

The eastern sun is red;
  The maiden like a bloom
  Follows me to my room.
  The maiden in my room
Follows me to the bed.

The eastern moon is bright;
  The maiden I adore
  Follows me out of doors.
  The maiden out of doors
Leaves me and goes out of sight.

Note: The maiden comes to the tryst like the eastern sun and leaves her lover like the eastern moon.

100. Disorder

Before the east sees dawn,
I put on clothes upside down.
O upside down I put them on,
For orders come from the ducal crown.

Before the east is bright,
I take the left sleeve for the right.
I put in the left sleeve my right arm,
For orders bring disorder and alarm.

Don't fence with feeble willow-tree!
The supervisor stares at me.
He takes night for day and I hate
To be too early or too late.

Note: This song is directed against the irregularity and disorder of the court of Qi. The officer, whom we suppose to be the writer, was not inattentive to his duties, but was hurriedly making preparations to attend the morning audience when a summons came to him out of time. The last stanza is metaphorical. A feeble fence served to mark out the forbidden ground, and even the most reckless paid regard to it; in the court of Qi, however, the evident distinction of morning and night was disregarded and times and seasons confounded.

101. Incest

— To Duke Xiang of Qi

The southern hill is great;
A male fox seeks his mate.
The way to Lu is plain;
Your sister with her train
Goes to wed Duke of Lu.
Why should you go there too?

The shoes are made in pairs,
And strings of gems she wears.
The way to Lu is plain;
Your sister goes to reign
And wed with Duke of Lu.
Why should you follow her too?

— To Duke Huan of Lu

For hemp the ground is ploughed and dressed
From north to south, from east to west.
When a wife comes to your household,
Your parents should be told.
If you told your father and mother,
Should your wife go back to her brother?

How is the firewood split?
An axe can sever it.
How can a wife be won?
With go-between it's done.
To be your wife she's vowed;
No incest is allowed.

Note: This is a satire against Duke Xiang of Qi and Duke Huan of Lu. In 708 BC Duke Huan married a daughter of Qi, known as Wen Jiang. There was an improper affection between her and her brother, Duke Xiang; and on his succession to Qi, the couple visited him. The consequences were incest between the brother and sister, the murder of the husband and a disgraceful connection, long continued, between the guilty pair. In the first stanza, the great southern hill alludes to the great State of Qi and the male fox seeking his mate alludes contemptuously to Duke Xiang seeking his sister who was going to wed Duke Huan of Lu. In the second stanza, the shoes and strings of gems made in pairs allude to the union of man and wife. In the third stanza, the ground well prepared for hemp alludes to the preparations for marriage between Duke Huan and Wen Jiang. In the last stanza, the splitting of firewood was a formality in contracting a marriage during the Zhou dynasty.

102. Longing

Don't till too large a ground,
Or weeds will spread around.
Don't miss one far away,
Or you'll grieve night and day.

Don't till too large a ground,
Or weeds will grow around.
Don't miss the far-off one,
Or your grief won't be done.

My son was young and fair
With his two tufts of hair.

Not seen for a short time,
He's grown up to his prime.

Note: A farmer who could not till a piece of ground too large for him longs
for his son who left home while young and could not come back for, though
grown up, he was in service.

103. Hunter and Hound

The bells of a hound
Give ringing sound;
Its master's mind
Is good and kind.

The good hound brings
Its double rings;
Its master's hair
Is curled and fair.

The good hound brings
Its triple rings;
Its master's beard
Is dèep revered.

Note: A woman thinks of her beloved hunter on hearing the bells of his
hound,

104. The Duchess of Qi

The basket is worn out
And fishes swim about.
The duchess comes with a crowd,
Capricious like the clouds.

The basket is worn out;
Bream and tench swim about.
The duchess comes like a flower,
Inconstant like the showers.

The basket is worn out;
Fish swim freely about.
Here comes the Duke of Qi's daughter,
Changeable like water.

Note: The worn-out basket unable to catch fish alludes to Duke Huan of Lu
unable to control the bold licentious conduct of his wife on returning to the
State of Qi (See song 101).

105. The Duchess of Lu

The duke's cab drives ahead
With screen of leather red;
The duchess starts on her way
Before the break of day.

The duke's steeds run amain;
Soft looks their hanging rein.
The duchess speeds on her way
At the break of the day.

The river flows along;
Travellers come in a throng.
Duke and duchess meet by day
And make merry all the way.

The river's overflowed
With travellers in a crowd;
Duke and duchess all day

Make merry all the way.

Note: This is a satire against the open shamelessness of Duchess Wen Jiang of Lu in her meeting with her brother, Duke Xiang of Qi. The merry-making may allude to their love-making. (See song 101)

106. The Archer Duke

Fairest of all,
He's grand and tall,
His forehead high
With sparkling eye;
He's fleet of foot
And skilled to shoot.

His fame is high,
With crystal eyes;
In brave array
He shoots all day;
Each shot a hit,
No son's so fit.

He's fair and bright
With keenest sight;
He dances well;
Each shot will tell;
Four shots right go;
He'll quell the foe.

Note: This song refers to Duke Zhuang of Lu, who, notwithstanding his beauty of person, elegance of manner and skill in archery, allowed his mother Wen Jiang to carry on her disgraceful connection with her brother, Duke Xiang of Qi, and himself joining the Duke of Qi in hunting, oblivious of his mother's shame and his father's murder. (See song 101)

(9) SONGS COLLECTED IN WEI

107. A Well-dressed Lady

In summer shoes with silken lace,
A maid walks on frost at a quick pace.
By slender fingers of the maid
Her mistress' beautiful attire is made.
The waistband and the collar fair
Are ready now for her mistress to wear.

The lady moves with pride;
She turns her head aside
With ivory pins in her hair.
Against her narrow mind
I'll use satire unkind.

Note: This is a satire against a well-dressed lady whose beautiful attire is
made by her maid who wears summer shoes in winter.

108. A Scholar Unknown

By the riverside, alas!
A scholar gathers grass.
He gathers grass at his leisure,
Graceful beyond measure.
Beyond measure his grace,
Why not in a high place?

By riverside picks he
The leaves of mulberry.
Amid the leaves he towers
As brilliant as the flowers.
Such brilliance and beauty,

Why not on official duty?

By riverside he trips
To gather the ox-lips.
His virtue not displayed
Like deeply buried jade.
Once his virtue appeared,
He would surpass his peers.

Note: This is a criticism of the State of Wei where only wealthy men could
be high officials while brilliant scholars could only gather grass and leaves
and had no official duties.

109. A Scholar Misunderstood

The fruit of peach tree
    Is used as food.
It saddens me
    To sing and brood.
Who knows me not
    Says I am proud.
He's right in what?
    Tell me aloud.
I'm full of woes;
    My heart would sink.
But no one knows,
    For none will think.

Of garden tree
    I eat the date.
It saddens me
    To roam the state.
Who knows me not
    Says I am queer.

He's right in what?
    O let me hear!
I'm full of woes;
    My heart would sink.
But no one knows,
    For none will think.

Note: This is another criticism of the State of Wei where unemployed poor
scholars ate peaches and dates.

110. A Homesick Soldier

I climb the hill covered with grass
    And look towards where my parents stay.
My father would say, "Alas!
    My son's on service far away;
    He cannot rest night and day.
O may he take good care
To come back and not remain there!"

I climb the hill devoid of grass
    And look towards where my parents stay.
My mother would say, "Alas!
    My youngest son's on service far away;
    He cannot sleep well night and day.
O may he take good care
To come back and not be captive there!"

I climb the hill-top green with grass
    And look towards where my brothers stay.
My eldest brother would say, "Alas!
    My youngest brother is on service far away;
    He stays with comrades night and day.
O may he take good care

To come back and not be killed there!''

Note: The service the soldier provided was exacted from the State of Wei by a more powerful State; in this service there was no place for patriotism and dignity. The song laments the poor and weak State of Wei whose men were torn from it to fight the battles of its oppressors.

111. Gathering Mulberry

Among ten acres of mulberry
All the planters are free.
Why not come back with me?

Beyond ten acres of mulberry
All the lasses are free.
O come away with me!

Note: This is a song sung by a planter of mulberry trees to a lass after gathering mulberries. According to another interpretation, a worthy officer, disgusted with the irregularities of the court, wants to withdraw from the public service to a quiet life among mulberry trees in the country.

112. The Woodcutter's Song

Chop, chop our blows on elm-trees go;
　　On rivershore we pile the wood.
The clear and rippling waters flow.
How can those who neither reap nor sow
Have three hundred sheaves of corn in their place?
How can those who nor hunt nor chase
Have in their courtyard badgers of each race?
　　Those lords are good
　　Who do not need work for food!

Chop, chop our blows for wheel-spokes go;
   On riverside we pile the wood.
The clear and even waters flow.
How can those who neither reap nor sow
Have three million sheaves in their place?
How can those who neither hunt nor chase
Have in their courtyard game of each race?
   Those lords are good
   Who need no work to eat their food!

Chop, chop our blows for the wheels go;
   At river brink we pile the wood.
The clear and dimpling waters flow.
How can those who neither reap nor sow
Have three hundred ricks of corn in their place?
How can those who neither hunt nor chase
Have in their courtyard winged games of each race?
   Those lords are good
   Who do not have to work for food!

Note: This is a song sung by a woodman while cutting wood or dancing,
against the idle and greedy ministers of the State of Wei.

113. To Corrupt Officials

Large rat, large rat,
   Eat no more millet we grow!
Three years you have grown fat.
   No care for us you show.
We'll leave you now, I swear,
   For a happier land,
A happier land where
   In our own place we'll stand.

Large rat, large rat,
Eat no more wheat we grow!
Three years you have grown fat.
No kindness to us you show.
We'll leave you now, I swear,
For a happier state,
A happier state where
We can decide our fate.

Large rat, large rat,
Eat no more rice we grow!
Three years you have grown fat.
No rewards to our labor go.
We'll leave you now, I swear,
For a happier plain,
A happier plain where
None will groan or complain.

Note: The large rat is symbolic of the corrupt official and the happy land is a Utopia of the peasants.

(10) SONGS COLLECTED IN TANG

114. Enjoy the Present

The cricket is chirping in the hall,
    The year will pass away.
The present is not enjoyed at all,
    We'll miss the passing day.
Do not enjoy to excess
    But do our duty with delight!
We'll enjoy ourselves none the less
    If we see those at left and right.

The cricket is chirping in the hall,
    The year will go away.
The present is not enjoyed at all,
    We'll miss the bygone day.
Do not enjoy to excess
    But only to the full extent!
We'll enjoy ourselves none the less
    If we are diligent.

Cricket chirping by the door,
    Our cart stands unemployed.
The year will be no more
    With the days unenjoyed.
Do not enjoy to excess
    But think of hidden sorrow!
We'll enjoy ourselves none the less
    If we think of tomorrow.

Note: This sings of the cheerfulness and discretion of the people of Jin and
their tempered enjoyment at fitting seasons.

115. Why Not Enjoy?

Uphill you have elm-trees;
  Downhill you have elms white.
You have dresses as you please.
  Why not wear them with delight?
You have horses and car.
  Why don't you take a ride?
One day when dead you are,
  Others will drive them with pride.

Uphill you've varnish trees,
  Downhill trees rooted deep.
You have rooms as you please.
  Why not clean them and sweep?
You have your drum and bell.
  Why don't you beat and ring?
One day when tolls your knell,
  Joy to others they'll bring.

Uphill you've chestnut trees,
  Downhill trees with deep root.
You have wine as you please.
  Why not play lyre and lute
To be cheerful and gay
  And to prolong your bloom?
When you are dead one day,
  Others will enter your room.

Note: This is a response to the previous song, bringing in the idea of death
to remove all hesitation in accepting the counsel to enjoyment there given.

116. Our Prince

The clear stream flows ahead
  And out the white rocks stand.
In our plain dress with collars red,
  We follow you to eastern land.
Shall we not rejoice since
We have seen our good prince?

The clear stream flows ahead
  And out the naked rocks stand.
In plain dress with sleeves broidered red,
  We follow you to northern land.
How can we feel sad since
We have seen our dear prince?

The clear stream flows along the border;
  Wave-beaten rocks stand out.
We've heard the secret order,
  But nothing should be talked about.

Note: The good prince refers to the uncle of Marquis Zhao of Jin, who was raised by a rebellious party to displace the marquis in 739 BC. The rocks are symbolic of the conspirators and the speaker was an adherent of the conspiracy who had heard the secret order to conspire against Marquis Zhao of Jin.

117. A Fertile Woman

The fruit of the pepper plant
Is so luxuriant.
The woman there
Is large beyond compare.
O pepper plant, extend
Your shoots without end!

The pepper plant there stands;
Its fruit will fill our hands.
The woman here
Is large without peer.
O pepper plant, extend
Your shoots without end!

Note: This song is supposed to celebrate the power and prosperity of the
good prince in the previous song, and to predict the growth of his family.
The pepper plant is so productive that the queen's bedroom was called pepper chamber since the Han dynasty in order that the queen might be as fertile as the plant.

118. A Wedding Song

The firewood's tightly bound
    When in the sky three stars appear.
What evening's coming round
    For me to find my bridegroom here!
O he is here! O he is here!
    What shall I not do with my dear!

The hay is tightly bound
    When o'er the house three stars appear.
What night is coming round
    To find by chance this couple here!
O they are here! O they are here!
    How lucky to see this couple dear!

The thorns are tightly bound
    When o'er the door three stars appear.
What midnight's coming round
    For me to find my beauty here!
O she is here! O she is here!

What shall I not do with my dear!

Note: The firewood or hay or thorns tightly bound allude to husband and wife well united. The three stars would be visible in the horizon on an autumnal evening, over the house at night and over the door at midnight. The first stanza should be sung by the bride, the second by the guests and the third by the bridegroom.

119. A Wanderer

A tree of russet pear
   Has leaves so thickly grown.
Alone I wander there
   With no friend of my own.
Is there no one
   Who would take care?
But there is none
Like my own father's son.
O wanderer, why are there few
To sympathize with you?
Can you not find another
To help you like a brother?

A tree of russet pear
   Has leaves so lushly grown.
Alone I loiter there
   Without a kinsman of my own.
Is there no one
   Who would take care of me?
But there is none
   Like my own family.
O loiterer, why are there few
To sympathize with you?
Can you not find another
To help you like a brother?

Note: This is a lament of a wanderer deprived of his brothers and relatives or forsaken by them. The tree covered by its leaves stands here in contrast with the wanderer desolate of friends.

120. An Unkind Chief

Lamb's fur and leopard's cuff,
To us you are so rough.
Can't we find another chief
Who would cause us no grief?

Lamb's fur and leopard's cuff,
You ne'er give us enough.
Can't we find another chief
Who would assuage our grief?

Note: The people complain of some high officer's hard treatment of them while they declare their loyalty. Line 1 in both stanzas indicate the officer's dress; lines 3 and 4 tell how the speakers may seek the lands of some other high officer, but that they feel an attachment to the family of their chief, and even to himself.

121. The Peasants' Complaint

Swish, swish sound the plumes of wild geese
Alighting on the bushy trees.
We must discharge the king's affairs.
How can we plant our millet with care?
On what can our parents rely?
O gods in boundless, endless sky,
When can we live in peace? I sigh.

Swish, swish flap the wings of wild geese
Alighting on the jujube trees.

We must discharge the king's affairs.
How can we plant our maize with care?
On what can our parents live and rely?
O gods in boundless, endless sky,
Can all this end before I die?

Swish, swish come the rows of wild geese,
Alighting on the mulberries.
We must discharge the king's affairs.
How can we plant our rice with care?
What can my parents have for food?
O Heavens good, O Heavens good!
When can we gain a livelihood?

Note: The men of Jin, called out to warfare by the king's order, mourn
over the consequent suffering of their parents, and long for their return to
their ordinary agricultural pursuits. The wild geese are said not to be fond of
alighting on trees, the attempt to perch occasioning them trouble and pain.
That is not the proper position for them; the speaker introduces them in this
position as metaphorical of the hardship of the soldiers' lot.

122. The Deceased Wife

Have I no dress?
    You made me seven.
I'm comfortless
    When you're in heaven.

Have I no dress?
    You made me six.
I'm comfortless
    As if on pricks.

Note: The poet is thinking of his deceased wife who made his dress.

123. Poverty

A lonely tree of russet pear
    Stands still on the left of the way.
O you for whom I care,
    Would you come as I pray?
In my heart you're so sweet.
When may I give you food to eat?

A lonely tree of russet pear
    Stands still on the right of the way.
O you for whom I care,
    Won't you come as I pray?
In my heart you're so good.
When may I give you food?

Note: Some one regrets the poverty of his circumstances, which prevented
him from gathering around him companions whom he admired. The lonely
tree would afford little or no shelter, and so the speaker sees in it a resem-
blance to his own condition.

124. Elegy

Vine grows o'er the thorn tree;
    Weeds in the field o'erspread.
    The man I love is dead.
Who'd dwell with me?

Vine grows o'er jujube tree;
    Weeds o'er the graveyard spread.
    The man I love is dead.
Who'd stay with me?

How fair the pillow of horn
    And the embroidered bed!

The man I love is dead.
Who'd stay with me till morn?

Long is the summer day;
   Cold winter night will loom.
I'd meet him in his tomb
When I have passed away.

Cold winter night will loom;
   Long is the summer day.
   When I have passed away,
We would dwell in the same tomb.

Note: This is the first elegy on one's deceased wife in Chinese literature. A widow mourns the death of her husband killed in the war waged by Duke Xian of Jin who reigned 675-650 BC. The vine supported by the tree may be suggestive of the widow's own desolate, unsupported condition or descriptive of the battleground where her husband had met his death.

125. Rumor

Could the sweet water plant be found
   On the top of the mountain high?
The rumor going round,
   If not believed, can't fly.
Put it aside, put it aside
   So that it can't prevail.
The rumor spreading far and wide
   Will be of no avail.

Could bitter water plant be found
   At the foot of the mountain high?
The rumor going round
   Is what we should deny.
Put it aside, put it aside

So that it can't prevail.
The rumor spreading far and wide
    Will be of no avail.

Could water plants be found
    East of the mountain high?
The rumor going round,
    If disregarded, will die.
Put it aside, put it aside
    So that it can't prevail.
The rumor spreading far and wide
    Will be of no avail.

Note: This song was directed against Duke Xian of Jin, who killed his son on the basis of rumors. Rumors should not be believed just as water plants cannot be found in the mountains.

(11) SONGS COLLECTED IN QIN

126. Enjoy Today!

The cab bells ring,
    Dappled steeds neigh,
"Let ushers bring
    In friends so gay!"

There're varnish trees uphill
    And chestnuts in the lowlands.
Friends see Lord Zhong sit still
    Before a lute-playing band.
"If we do not enjoy today,
At eighty joy will pass away."

There're mulberries uphill
    And willows in lowlands.
Friends see Lord Zhong sit still
    Beside his music band.
"If we do not enjoy today,
We'll regret when life ebbs away."

Note: This song celebrates the pleasures of Lord Zhong of Qin, who, made
a great officer of the court by King Xuan in 826 BC, began to turn Qin
from a barbarian State to a music-loving civilized one. China was eventual-
ly unified under the reign of the Empire of Qin in 221 BC.

127. Winter Hunting

Holding in hand six reins
    Of four iron-black steeds,
Our lord hunts on the plains
    With good hunters he leads.

The male and female preys
    Have grown to sizes fit.
"Shoot at the left!" he says;
    Their arrows go and hit.

He comes to northern park
    With his four steeds at leisure;
Long- and short-mouthed hounds bark
    In the carriage of pleasure.

Note: The song celebrates the growing opulence of Duke Xiang of Qin, raised to the rank of earl by King Ping and assuming the style becoming his rank in 769 BC.

128. A Lord on Expedition

His chariot finely bound,
Crisscrossed with straps around,
Covered with tiger's skin,
Driven by horses twin;
His steeds controlled with reins
Through slip rings like gilt chains;
I think of my lord dear
Far-off on the frontier;
He's pure as jade and plain.
O my heart throbs with pain.

His four fine steeds there stand;
He holds six reins in hand.
The insides have black mane,
Yellow the outside twain.
Dragon shields on two wings,
Buckled up as with strings.
I think of my lord dear

So good on the frontier.
When will he come to me?
Can I be yearning-free?

How fine his team appears!
How bright his trident spears!
His shield bears a carved face;
In tiger's skin bow-case
With bamboo frames and bound
With strings, two bows are found.
I think of my dear mate,
Rise early and sleep late.
   My dear, dear one,
Can I forget the good you've done?

Note: The wife of a lord absent on an expedition against the western tribe,
by whom King You of Zhou was killed in 771 BC, gives a glowing description of his chariot and praises him, expressing her regret at his absence.

129. The Fair One

The reeds grow green;
   Frosted dew-drops gleam.
Where can she be seen?
   Beyond the stream.
Upstream I go;
   The way's so long.
And downstream, lo!
   She's thereamong.

The reeds turn white,
   Dew not yet dried.
Where's she so bright?
   On the other side.

Upstream I go;
   Hard is the way.
And downstream, lo!
   She's far away.

The reeds still there,
   With frost dews blend.
Where's she so fair?
   At the river's end.
Upstream I go;
   The way does wind.
And downstream, lo!
   She's far behind.

Note: This is the first symbolic poem in Chinese literature. The fair one is symbolic of the ideal the poet is seeking after.

130. The Southern Hill

What's on the southern hill?
   There're mume trees and white firs.
Our lord comes and stands still,
   Wearing a robe and furs.
Vermillion is his face.
O what majestic grace!

What's on the southern hill?
   There are trees of white pears.
Our lord comes and stands still;
   A broidered robe he wears.
His gems give tinkling sound.
May he live long and sound!

Note: This song celebrates the dignity of Duke Xiang of Qin, the first of the chiefs of Qin to be recognized as a prince of the kingdom. Wearing the robe of a duke, conferred by King Ping in 760 BC after his victory over the western tribes, he passed by the Southern Mountains on his way west to Qin.

131. Burial of Three Worthies

The golden orioles flew
    And lit on jujube tree.
Who's buried with Duke Mu?
    The eldest of the three.
This eldest worthy son
Could be rivaled by none.
Coming to the graveside,
Who'd not be terrified?
O good Heavens on high,
Why should the worthy die?
If he could live again,
Who would not have been slain?

The golden oriole flew
    And lit on a mulberry.
Who's buried with Duke Mu?
    The second of the three.
The second worthy son
Could be equalled by none.
Coming to the graveside,
Who'd not be terrified?
O good Heavens on high,
Why should the worthy die?
If he could live again,
Who would not have been slain?

The golden oriole flew
    And lit on the thorn tree.

Who's buried with Duke Mu?
   The youngest of the three.
The youngest worthy son
Could be surpassed by none.
Coming to the graveside,
Who'd not be terrified?
O good Heavens on high,
Why should the worthy die?
If he could live again,
Who would not have been slain?

Note: Three worthies were buried alive in the same grave with Duke Mu of
Qin in 620 BC. They were not so free as the golden oriole.

132. The Forgotten

The falcon flies above
   To the thick northern wood.
While I see not my love,
   I'm in a gloomy mood.
How can it be my lot
To be so much forgot?

The bushy oaks above
   And six elm-trees below.
While I see not my love,
   There is no joy of know.
How can it be my lot
   To be so much forgot?

The sparrow-plums above,
   Below trees without leaf.
While I see not my love,
   My heart is drunk with grief.

How can it be my lot
To be so much forgot?

Note: On seeing the falcon flying against the wind to the northern wood of oaks, elms and plums, a wife tells her grief because her husband has forgotten to come home as the falcon does.

133. Comradeship

Are you not battle-drest?
Let's share the plate for breast!
We shall go up the line.
Let's make our lances shine!
Your foe is mine.

Are you not battle-drest?
Let's share the coat and vest!
We shall go up the line.
Let's make our halberds shine!
Your job is mine.

Are you not battle-drest?
Let's share the kilt and the rest!
We shall go up the line.
Let's make our armor shine!
We'll march your hand in mine.

Note: This is the song sung by Duke Ai of Qin when he despatched five hundred chariots to the rescue of the State of Chu besieged by Wu in 505 BC. In this song the soldiers of Qin declare their readiness and encourage one another to fight in the king's cause.

134. Duke Wen of Jin

I see my uncle dear
  Off north of River Wei.
What's the gift for one I revere?
  Golden cab with steeds bay.

I see my uncle dear
  Off and think of my mother.
What's the gift for one she and I revere?
  Jewels and gems for her brother.

Note: The famous Duke Wen of Jin took refuge in the State of Qin for nineteen long years and was restored to his native State with the help of his cousin, Duke Mu of Qin. Duke Kang was then the heir-apparent of Qin and escorted his uncle into the State of Jin when he undertook his expedition to re-
cover it. This song expresses the feeling with which Duke Kang escorted him
to Jin.

135. The Impoverished

Ah me! Where is my house of yore?
  Now I 've not a great deal
  To eat at every meal.
Alas! I can 't live as before.

Ah me! Where are my dishes four?
  Now hungry I feel
  At every meal.
Alas! I can 't eat as before.

Note:Note: It is said that in this song some old servant of Duke Mu complains of the diminished respect and attention paid to him by his successor,
Duke Kang.

(12) SONGS COLLECTED IN CHEN

136. A Bewitching Dancer

In the highland above
   You dance with swing.
With you I fall in love,
   Hopeless I sing.

You beat the drum
   At the foot of the highland.
Winter and summer come,
   You dance, a plume in hand.

You beat a vessel round
   On the way to the highland.
Spring or fall comes around,
   You dance, a fan in hand.

Note: The highland was a favorite resort of pleasure-seekers in the chief city
of Chen. The vessel was an earthernware used for holding wine and drawing
water, and also for a primitive instrument of music. The plume or plumes, either single or formed into fans, was carried by the dancer and waved in harmony with the movements of the body.

137. Dancers

From white elms at the east gate
   To oak-trees on the mound
Lad and lass have a date;
   They dance gaily around.

A good morning is chosen

To go to the south where,
Leaving the hemp unwoven,
    They dance at a country fair.

They go at morning hours
    Together to the highland.
O you look like sunflowers,
    A token of love in hand.

Note : This is a love song of hemp-weavers. Line 3 of the last stanza is directly addressed to the lasses.

138. Contentment

Beneath my door of single beam
    I can sit and rest at my leisure;
Beside the gently flowing stream
    I drink to stay hunger with pleasure.

If you want to eat fish,
Why must you have bream as you wish?
If you want to be wed,
Must you have Qi, the nobly bred?

If you want to eat fish,
Why must you have carp as you wish?
If you want to be wed,
Must you have Song, the highly bred?

Note: This song describes the contentment and happiness of a poor recluse. The door of single beam is an apology for a door, one piece of wood placed across the opening in a hut or hermitage, under whose roof one can still enjoy oneself and forget one's hunger. As bream or carp is hard to come by; one might be satisfied with fish of smaller note. And so, one could be happy with a wife, though she were not a noble Qi or Song.

139. To a Good Maiden

At eastern gate we could
  Steep hemp in the river long.
O maiden fair and good,
  To you I'll sing a song.

At eastern gate we could
  Steep nettle in the creek.
O maiden fair and good,
  To you I wish to speak.

At eastern gate we could
  Steep in the moat rush-rope.
O maiden fair and good,
  On you I hang my hope.

Note: This is a love song sung by a hemp-weaver to a maiden along the moat surrounding the city wall. The stalks of the hemp have to be steeped, preparatory to getting the threads from them. Strings and ropes can be made from the fibres of the long leaf.

140. A Date

On poplars by the eastern gate
  The leaves are rustling light.
At dusk we have a date;
  The evening star shines bright.

On poplars by the eastern gate
  The leaves are shivering.
At dusk we have a date;
  The morning star is quivering.

Note: The shivering leaves and the quivering star may hint at the love-
making beneath the poplar tree by the eastern gate of the chief city of Chen.

141. An Evil-Doer

At burial gate there's thorn.
  Strike with your axe a blow!
A man is evil born,
  Which all the people know.
But he won't give it o'er
And will act as before.

At burial gate there's jujube tree,
  On which owls perch all the day long.
The man from evil is not free;
  I'll warn him by singing a song.
But he won't listen to my plea
  For he cannot tell right from wrong.

Note: This is a satirical song directed against Tuo of Chen, a brother of
Duke Huan (743-706 BC), upon whose death Tuo killed his eldest son and
got possession of the State of Chen, coming to an untimely end himself the
year after. The thorns at the burial gate and the owls perching on the jujube
tree were both evil omens, and are employed to introduce the subject of the
song. It is said this song was sung by a mulberry-gathering woman to ward
off an official's attempt to rape her.

142. The Evil Tongue

Can magpies on the stream appear
  Or water grass on hillock grow?
Believe none who deceive, my dear,
  Or my heart will be full of woe.

Can temple court be paved with tiles and bricks
   Or hillock spread with water grass?
Believe, my dear, none who play tricks
   Or I'll worry for you, alas!

Note: A woman laments the alienation of her lover by means of evil tongues. Magpies should no more appear on the stream than water grass on hillock, nor should the temple court be paved with tiles and bricks.

143. The Moon

The moon shines bright;
My love's snow-white.
She looks so cute.
Can I be mute?

The bright moon gleams;
My dear love beams.
Her face so fair,
Can I not care?

The bright moon turns;
With love she burns.
Her hands so fine,
Can I not pine?

Note: This is the earliest Chinese serenade sung under moonlight. The lover tells the excitement of his desire for a beautiful maiden. He is supposed to be led on from his view of the moon to speak of the object of his affections.

144. The Duke's Mistress

Why goes he to the wood?
　　After his mistress' son?
He cares not for the wood
　　But for his fairest one.

"I drive to the neighborhood
　　And take a short rest there.
I'll ride then to the wood
　　And pass a night with the fair."

Note: The song was directed against the intrigue of Duke Ling of Chen (612-598 BC) with the beautiful Lady Xia. The duke went to the countryside to meet her under the pretext of visiting her son Xia Nan, by whom he was killed in 598 BC.

145. A Lovesick Lady

By poolside over there
　　Grow reed and lotus bloom.
There is a lady fair
　　Lovesick and full of gloom.
She does nothing in bed;
Like streams her tears are shed.

By poolside over there
　　Grow reed and orchid bloom.
There is a lady fair,
　　Whose heart is full of gloom.
Tall and with a curled head,
She does nothing in bed.

By poolside over there
Grow reed and lotus thin.
There is a lady fair,
    Tall and with double chin.
She does nothing in bed,
Tossing about her head.

Note: It is said that this song describes the betwitching Lady Xia mourning over the death of Duke Ling of Chen and her son Xia Nan killed by King Zhuang of Chu in 598 BC (See song 144). It is also said that this song describes a lady's longing for some one she met by the side of the lotus pool.

(13) SONGS COLLECTED IN GUI

146. The Lord of Gui

You seek amusement in official dress;
　　You hold your court in sacrificial gown.
How can we not think of you in distress?
　　O how can our heavy heart not sink down!

You find amusement in your lamb's fur dress;
　　In your fox's fur at court you appear.
How can we not think of you in distress?
　　O how can our heart not feel sad and drear!

You appear in your greasy dress
　　Which glistens in the sun.
How can we not think of you in distress?
　　To see the wrong you have done!

Note: The lord of Gui, fond of sumptuous official dress, did not hold his
court and the State of Gui was extinguished in 769 BC.

147. The Mourner

The mourner's white cap seen,
The mourner looks so lean;
I feel a sorrow keen.

Seeing the mourner's white dress,
I become comfortless;
I would share his distress.

I see his white cover-knee,
Sorrow is knotted on me,
One with him I would be.

Note: The speaker expresses his sympathy with the mourner in white cap,
dress and cover-knee, a sort of leather apron covering the knee, also the accompaniment of the white cap and dress.

148. The Unconscious Tree

In lowlands grows the cherry
    With branches swaying in high glee.
Why do you look so merry?
    I envy you, unconscious tree.

In lowlands grows the cherry
    With flowers blooming in the breeze.
Why do you look so merry?
    I envy you for homeless ease.

In lowlands grows the cherry
    With fruit overloading the tree.
Why do you look so merry?
    I envy you from cares so free.

Note: Some one groaning under the oppression of the government wishes he
were free from envy and family cares as an unconscious cherry tree.

149. Nostalgia

The wind blows a strong blast;
The carriage's running fast.
I look to homeward way.
Who can my grief allay?

The whirlwind blows a blast;
The cab runs wild and fast.
Looking to backward way,
Can I not pine away?

Who can boil fish?
I'll wash their boiler as they wish.
Who's going west?
Will he bring words at my request?

Note: King Ping removed to the east in 769 BC and an officer of the State
of Gui followed him in a cab because his homeland was destroyed by Duke
Wu of Zheng. The officer wished his State be restored so that he might go
west to boil fish. By "words" he might mean this song he had made.

(14) SONGS COLLECTED IN CAO

150. The Ephemera

The ephemera's wings
　Like morning robes are bright.
Grief to my heart it brings:
　Where will it be at night?

The ephemera's wings
　Like rainbow robes are bright.
Grief to my heart it brings:
　Where will it go by night?

The ephemera's hole
　Like robe of hemp snow-white.
It brings grief to my soul:
　Where may I rest tonight?

Note: This song was directed against Duke Zhao (reigned 661－651 BC) of
the small State of Cao, who was occupied with frivolous pleasures and oblivious of important matters. The State of Cao was extinguished by Duke Jing
of Song in 487 BC.

151. The Poor and the Rich

The poor attendants hold spears
　And halberds to escort;
The rich three hundred peers
　Wearing red cover-knee at court.

The pelican appears
　But its wings are not wet;

Unworthy are those peers
    Of the rich dress they get.

The pelican appears
    Without wetting its beak;
Unworthy are those peers
    Of the favor they seek.

At sunrise o'er south hill
    The attendants still wait;
Their fair daughters feel ill
    At home from hunger great.

Note: This is a lament over the favor shown to three hundred worthless officers at the court of Duke Gong of Cao (651-617 BC), and the
discountenance of the attendants in charge of reception of guests. The pelican contriving somehow to get its food without effort or labor of its own re-
sembles the useless officers who had their salaries and positions without
doing anything for them.

152. Our Good Lord

The cuckoo in the mulberries
Breed seven fledglings with ease.
Our good lord should take care
To deal with all fair and square.
He treats all fair and square;
His heart is good beyond compare.

The cuckoos in the mulberries
Breed fledglings in mume trees.
Our good lord's fair and bright,
His girdle hemmed with silk white.
His girdle has silk hems,
Adorned with jade and gems.

The cuckoos in the mulberries
Breed fledglings in the jujube trees.
Our lord is a good one;
Nothing wrong has he done.
He's a good magistrate,
A model for the state.

The cuckoos in the mulberries
Breed fledglings in the hazel trees.
Our lord is a good magistrate
To help the people of the state.
He helps people to right the wrong.
May he live ten thousand years long!

Note: The good lord is an ideal ruler and is celebrated, in contrast with the
ruler of Cao.

153. The Capital

The busy grass drowned by
    Cold water flowing down,
When I awake, I sigh
    For our capital town.

The southernwood drowned by
    Cold water flowing down,
When I awake, I sigh
    For our municipal town.

The bushy plants drowned by
    Cold water flowing down,
When I awake, I sigh
    For our old royal town,

Where millet grew in spring,
    Enriched by happy rain;
The state ruled by a wise king
    And toilers had their grain.

Note: The bushy grass and plants drowned in cold water allude to the small State of Cao drowned in misery, which made the writer think of the capital, municipal and royal towns of Zhou and their prosperity.

(15) SONGS COLLECTED IN BIN

154. Life of Peasants

In seventh moon Fire Star west goes;
  In ninth to make dresses we are told.
In eleventh moon the wind blows;
  In twelfth the weather's cold.
We have no garments warm to wear.
  How can we get through the year?
In the first moon we mend our plough with care;
  In the second our way afield we steer.
Our wives and children take the food
To southern fields; the overseer says, "good!"

In seventh moon Fire Star west goes;
  In ninth we make dresses all day long.
By and by warm spring grows
  And golden orioles sing their song.
The lasses take their baskets deep
  And go along the small pathways
To gather tender mulberry leaves in heap.
  When lengthen the vernal days,
They pile in heaps the southernwood,
Their heart in gloomy mood,
For they will say adieu to maidenhood.

In seventh moon Fire Star west goes;
  In eighth we gather rush and reed.
In silkworm month with axe's blows
  We cut mulberry sprigs with speed.
We lop off branches long and high
  And bring young tender leaves in.
In seventh moon we hear shrikes cry;

In eighth moon we begin to spin.
We use a bright red dye
    And a dark yellow one
    To color robes of our lord's son.

In fourth moon grass begins to seed;
    In fifth cicadas cry.
In eighth moon to reap we proceed;
    In tenth down come leaves dry.
In eleventh moon we go in chase
    For wild cats and foxes fleet
To make furs for the son of noble race.
    In the twelfth moon we meet
And manoeuvre with lance and sword.
We keep the smaller boars for our reward
And offer larger ones o'er to our lord.

In fifth moon locusts move their legs;
    In sixth the spinner shakes its wings.
In seventh in the field laying its eggs,
    In eighth under the eaves the cricket sings.
In ninth it moves indoors when chilled;
    In tenth it enters under the bed.
We clear the corners, chinks are filled,
    We smoke the house and rats run in dread.
We plaster northern window and door
    And tell our wives and lad and lass:
The old year will soon be no more.
    Let's dwell inside, alas!

In sixth moon we've wild plums and grapes to eat;
    In seventh we cook beans and mallows nice.
In eighth moon down the dates we beat;
    In tenth we reap the rice
And brew the vernal wine,

A cordial for the oldest-grown.
In seventh moon we eat melon fine;
   In eighth moon the gourds are cut down.
In ninth we gather the hemp-seed;
   Of withered trees we make firewood;
We gather lettuce to feed
   Our husbandmen as food.

In ninth moon we repair the threshing-floor;
   In tenth we bring in harvest clean:
The millets early sown and late are put in store,
   And wheat and hemp, paddy and bean.
There is no rest for husbandmen:
   Once harvesting is done, alas!
We're sent to work in lord's house then.
   By day for thatch we gather reed and grass;
At night we twist them into ropes,
   Then hurry to mend the roofs again,
For we should not abandon the hopes
   Of sowing in time our fields with grain.

In the twelfth moon we hew out ice;
   In the first moon we store it deep.
In the second we offer early sacrifice
   Of garlic, lamb and sheep.
In ninth moon frosty is the weather;
   In tenth we sweep and clear the threshing-floor.
We drink two bottles of wine together
   And kill a lamb before the door.
Then we go up
   To the hall where
We raise our buffalo-horn cup
   And wish our lord to live fore'er.

Note: This is a description of the life of the peasants in Bin, where the first
settlers of the House of Zhou dwelt for nearly five centuries from 1796 to

1325 BC. The specification of the months is according to the calendar of the Xia dynasty (2205 – 1766 BC).

155. A Mother Bird

Owl, owl, you've taken my young ones away.
  Do not destroy my nest!
With love and pains I toiled all day
  To hatch them without rest.

Before it is going to rain,
  I gather roots of mulberry
And mend my nest with might and main
  Lest others bully me.

My claws feel sore
  From gathering reeds without rest;
I put them up in store
  Until my beak feels pain to mend my nest.

Sparse is my feather
  And torn my tail.
My nest is tossed in stormy weather;
  I cry and wail to no avail:
Owl, owl, do not destroy my nest,
Or I shall have nowhere to rest!

Note: This is the earliest fable in Chinese literature. The Duke of Zhou, regent in 1115 BC, in the character of a mother bird whose young ones have been destroyed by an owl, vindicates the decisive course he had taken with rebellion. Two of his brothers, who had been associated with Wu Geng, son of the dethroned king of Shang in charge of the territory which had been left to him by King Wu, joined him in rebellion, having first spread a rumor impeaching the fidelity of the duke to his nephew, the young King Cheng. He took the field against them, put to death Wu Geng and dealt with his brothers according to the measure of their guilt.

156. A Home-coming Warrior

To east hills sent away,
　　Long did I there remain.
Now on my westward way,
　　There falls a drizzling rain.
I come back from the east;
　　My heart yearns for the west.
Fighting no more at least,
　　I'll wear a farmer's vest.
Curled up as silkworms crept
　　On the mulberry leaves,
Beneath my cart alone I slept.
　　How my heart grieves!

To east hills sent away,
　　Long did I there remain.
Now on my westward way,
　　There falls a drizzling rain.
The vine of gourd may clamber
　　The wall and eave all o'er;
I may find woodlice in my chamber
　　And cobwebs across the door;
I may see in paddock deer-track
　　And glow-worms' fitful light.
Still I long to be back
　　To see such sorry sight.

To east hills sent away,
　　Long did I there remain.
Now on my westward way,
　　There falls a drizzling rain.
The cranes on ant-hill cry;
　　My wife in cottage room
May sprinkle, sweep and sigh

For my returning home.
The gourd may still hang high
    Beside the tall chestnut tree.
Oh! three years have gone by
    Since last she was with me.

To east hills sent away,
    Long did I there remain.
Now on my westward way,
    There falls a drizzling rain.
The oriole takes flight
    With glinting wings outspread.
I remember on horses white
    My bride came to be wed.
Her sash by her mother tied,
    She should observe the rite.
Happy was I to meet my bride;
    How happy I' ll be with my wife in sight!

Note: A soldier under the Duke of Zhou tells of his toils in the expedition to
the east in 1115 BC (See Note on song 155) and on his return, of his appre-
hensions and his joy at the last.

157. With Broken Axe

With broken axe in hand
    And hatchet, our poor mates
Follow our duke from eastern land;
    We' ve conquered the four States.
Alas! those who are not strong
Enough cannot come along.

With broken axe in hand
    And chisel, our poor mates

Follow our duke from eastern land;
  We' ve controlled the four States.
Alas! those who do not survive!
Lucky those still alive!

With broken axe in hand
  And halberd, our poor mates
Follow our duke from eastern land;
  We' ve ruled o' er the four States.
Alas! those who are dead!
Lucky, let's go ahead!

Note: In 1025 BC the Duke of Zhou undertook an expedition against the four eastern States ruled by his own brothers Guan and Cai and the son of the last king of Shang. The battles were so fierce that many axes and hatchets were broken, and it took him three years to put down the rebellion.

158. Song of a Bridegroom

Do you know how to make
  An axe-handle? With an axe keen.
Do you know how to take
  A wife? Please ask a go-between.

When a handle is hewed,
  The pattern should not be far.
When a maiden is wooed,
  See how many betrothal gifts there are!

Note: This is a song sung by a bridegroom to give counsel to his unmarried friends. An important principle is derived by Confucius from the first two lines of the second stanza that the rule for man's way of life is in himself, or while there is a proper way for everything, man need not go far to find out what it is.

159. The Duke's Return

In the nine-bagged net
   There are bream and red-eye.
See ducal coronet
   And gown on which embroidered dragons fly.

Along the shore the swan's in flight.
Where will our duke alight?
He stops with us only tonight.

The swan's in flight along the track.
Our duke, once gone, will not come back.
His soldiers pass the night in bivouac.

Let's keep his broidered gown!
May he not leave our town
Lest in regret our hearts will drown!

Note: The people of the eastern States express their admiration for the Duke
of Zhou, and sorrow at his returning to the west. The net in question was
composed somehow of nine bags or compartments. Both the bream and the
red-eye are good fish, and the writer therefore passes on from them to speak
of the good Duke of Zhou. The flying dragon was an emblematic figure of
rank depicted on the ducal robe.

160. An Old Wolf

The wolf springs forward on his dewlap
   And trips back on his tail.
The big-bellied lord in the trap
   Struggles in slippers red to no avail.

The wolf trips back upon his tail
   And springs forward on his dewlap.
The ill-famed lord struggles to no avail
   To free himself of the trap.

Another Version

The duke can't go ahead
   Nor at his ease retreat.
He's good to put on slippers red
   And leave the regent's seat.

The duke cannot retreat
   Nor with ease forward go.
He's good to leave his seat
   And keep his fame aglow.

Note: The wolf in the text is supposed to be an old wolf, whose dewlap and tail have grown to a very large size. He is further supposed to be taken in a pit, and to be making frantic efforts to escape, all in vain, for his own dewlap and tail are in his way. The first version is a satire on a lord, and in the second the old wolf is symbolic of the Duke of Zhou (as regent) in a dilemma, for if he should advance, the rumor would spread that he would seize the throne; if he should retreat, the young king might be dethroned. The duke left the regent's seat in 1109 BC.

Part II

Book of Odes

Part II

Book of Odes

(16) FIRST DECADE OF ODES

161. To Guests

How gaily call the deer
  While grazing in the shade!
I have welcome guests here.
  Let lute and pipe be played!
Let offerings appear
  And lute and strings vibrate!
If you love me, friends dear,
  Help me to rule the state!

How gaily call the deer
  While eating southernwood!
I have welcome guests here

  Who give advices good.
O you are so benign,
  My people will learn from you.
I have delicious wine,
  You may enjoy my brew.

How gaily call the deer
  Eating grass in the shade!
I have welcome guests here.
  Let lute and flute be played!
Play lute and zither fine,
  We may enjoy our best.
I have delicious wine
  To delight the heart of my guest.

Note: This is a festal ode sung at entertainments to the king's guests from
the feudal States. It refers to the time of King Wen (1184 – 1134 BC).

162. Filial Piety

Four horses forward go
   Along a winding way.
How can my homesickness not grow?
   But the king's affairs bear no delay.
My heart is full of woe.

Four horses forward go;
   They pant and snort and neigh.
How can my homesickness not grow?
   But the king's affairs bear no delay.
I can't rest or drive slow.

Doves fly from far and near
   Up and down on their way.
They may rest on oaks with their peers,
   But the king's affairs bear no delay,
And I can't serve my father dear.

Doves fly from far and near,
   High and low on their way.
They may perch on trees with their peers,
   But the king's affairs bear no delay,
And I can't serve my mother dear.

I drive a black-maned white steed
   And hurry on my way.
Don't I wish to go home with speed?
   I can't but sing this lay
Though I have my mother to feed.

Note: This is a festal ode, complimentary to an officer on his return from an expedition, celebrating the union in him of royal duty and filial feeling.

163. The Envoy

The flowers look so bright
On lowland and on height.
The envoy takes good care
To visit people here and there.

"My ponies have brown manes
And smooth are the six reins.
I ride them here and there,
Making inquiries everywhere.

"My horses have white manes;
Silken are the six reins.
I ride them here and there,
Seeking counsel everywhere.

"My horses have black manes;
Glossy are the six reins.
I ride them here and there,
Seeking advice everywhere.

"My horses have grey manes;
Shiny are the six reins.
I ride them here and there,
Visiting people everywhere."

Note: This is an ode appropriate to the despatches of an envoy and the discharge of his duties.

164. Brotherhood

The blooms of cherry tree,
　　How gorgeous they appear!
Great as the world my be,
　　As brother none's so dear.

A dead man will be brought
　　To brother's mind with woe.
A lost man will be sought
　　By brothers high and low.

When a man is in need,
　　Like wagtails flying high
To help him brothers speed,
　　While good friends only sigh.

Brothers may fight within;
　　They fight the foe outside.
Good friends are not kin:
　　They only stand aside.

When war comes to an end,
　　Peace and rest reappear.
Some may think a good friend
　　Better than brothers dear.

But you may drink your fill
　　With dishes in array
And feel happier still
　　To drink with brothers gay.

Your union with your wife
　　Is like music of lutes

And with brothers your life
 Has longer, deeper roots.

Delight your family,
 Your wife and children dear!
If farther you can see,
 Happiness will be near.

Note: This ode was for use at entertainments given at the court to the
princes with the same surname as the royal House.

165. Friendship and Kinship

The blows on brushwood go
 While the songs of the bird
From the deep vale below
 To lofty trees are heard.
Long, long the bird will sing
 And for an echo wait;
Even though on the wing,
 It tries to seek a mate.
We're more than what it is,
 Can we not seek a friend?
If gods listen to this,
 There'll be peace in the end.

Heighho, they fell the wood;
 I have strained off my wine.
My fatted lamb is good;
 I'll ask kinsmen to dine.
Send them my best regards
 Lest they resist my wishes;
Sprinkle and sweep the yards
 And arrange eight round dishes!

Since I have fatted meat,
     I'll invite kinsmen dear.
Why won't they come to eat?
     Can't they find pleasure here?

On brushwood go the blows;
     I have strained off my wine.
The dishes stand in rows;
     All brethren come to dine.
Men may quarrel o'er food,
     O'er early or late brew.
Drink good wine if you could,
     Or o'ernight brew will do.
Let us beat drums with pleasure
     And dance to music fine!
Whenever we have leisure,
     Let's drink delicious wine!

Note: This is a festal ode sung when entertaining friends living in the woods.

166. The Royalty

May Heaven bless our king
     With great security,
Give him favor and bring
     Him great felicity
That he may do more good
And people have more food!

May Heaven bless our king
     With perfect happiness,
Make him do everything
     Right and with great success

That he may have his will
And we enjoy our fill!

May Heaven bless our king
  With great prosperity
Like hills and plains in spring
  Grown to immensity
Or the o'erbrimming river
Flowing forever and ever!

Offer your wine and rice
  From summer, fall to spring
As filial sacrifice
  To your ancestral king
Whose soul in the witch appears:
"May you live long, long years!"

The spirit comes and confers
  Many blessings on you
And on simple laborers
  But daily food and brew.
The common people raise
Their voice to sing your praise:

"Like the moon in the sky
  Or sunrise over the plain,
Like southern mountains high
  Which never fall or wane
Or like luxuriant pines, —
May such be your succeeding lines!"

Note: The guests feasted by the king praise him and desire for him the blessing of Heaven and his ancestors, whose souls were supposed to appear in the witch.

167. A Homesick Warrior

We gather fern
  Which springs up here.
Why not return
  Now ends the year?
We left dear ones
To fight the Huns.
We wake all night:
The Huns cause fright.

We gather fern
  So tender here.
Why not return?
  My heart feels drear:
Hard pressed by thirst
And hunger worst,
My heart is burning
For home I'm yearning.
Far from home, how
To send word now?

We gather fern
  Which grows tough here.
Why not return?
  The tenth month's near.
The war not won,
  We cannot rest.
Consoled by none,
  We feel distressed.

How gorgeous are
  The cherry flowers!
How great the car
  Of that lord of ours!

It's driven by
  Four horses nice.
We can't but hie
  In one month thrice.

Driven by four
  Horses alined,
Our lord before,
  We march behind.
Four horses neigh,
  Quiver and bow
Ready each day
  To fight the foe.

When I left here,
Willows shed tear.
I come back now;
Snow bends the bough.
Long, long the way;
Hard, hard the day.
My grief o'erflows.
Who knows? Who knows?

Note: This and the next two odes form a triad, all referring to an expedition
undertaken in the time of King Wen, when he was still Duke of Zhou under
the last king of the Shang dynasty.

168. General Nan Zhong and His Wife

Out goes my car
  To the countryside.
Ordered we are
  To march and ride.

The drivers make
　　Ready the horses.
The state is at stake,
　　Let's use our forces!

Out goes my car
　　Far from the town.
Adorned flags are
　　With falcons brown,
Turtles and snakes;
　　They fly in flurry.
O my heart aches
　　And my men worry.

Ordered am I
　　To build a north wall.
Cars seem to fly;
　　Flags rise and fall.
I'm going forth,
　　Leading brave sons,
To wall the north
　　And beat the Huns.

On parting day
　　Millets in flower.
On westward way
　　It snows in shower.
The state is at stake,
　　I can't leave borders.
My heart would ache
　　At royal orders.

Hear insects sing;
See hoppers spring!
My lord not seen,

My grief is keen.
I see him now;
Grief leaves my brow.
With feats aglow,
He's beat the foe.

Long, long this spring,
  Green, green the grasses.
Hear orioles sing;
  See busy lasses!
With captive crowd,
  Still battle-drest,
My lord looks proud:
  He's beat the west.

Note: This and the last ode are the earliest frontier poems in Chinese literature. General Nan Zhong is the speaker in the first four stanzas and his wife
in the last two. Some critics refer this triad to the time of King Xuan
(826 – 781 BC).

169. A Soldier's Wife

Lonely stands the pear tree
  With rich fruit on display.
From the king's affairs not free,
  He's busy day by day.
The tenth moon's drawing near,
  A soldier's wife, I feel drear,
My husband is not here.

Lonely stands the pear tree;
  So lush its leaves appear.
From the king's affairs he's not free,
  My heart feels sad and drear.
So luch the plants appear,

A soldier's wife, I feel drear:
Where is my husband dear?

I gather fruit from medlar tree
   Upon the northern hill.
From the king's affairs he's not free,
   Our parents rue their fill.
See that shabby car appear
   With horses weary and drear!
My soldier must be near.

No man nor car appear;
My heart feels sad and drear.
Alas! you're overdue.
Can I not long for you?
The fortune-tellers say:
You must be on your way.
But why should you delay?

Note: This is a description of the anxiety and longing of a soldier's wife for
his return from the expedition against the Huns. The first stanza is in autumn, the second in spring and the last two in another autumn.

170. A Feast

The fish in the basket are fine:
   Sand-blowers and yellow-jaws as food.
Our host has wine
   So abundant and good.

The fish in the basket are fine:
   So many tenches and breams.
Our host has wine:
   So good and abundant it seems.

The fish in the basket are fine:
  So many carps and mud-fish.
Our host has wine
  As abundant as you wish.

How abundant the food
So delicious and good!

How delicious the food at hand
From the sea and the land!

We love the food with reason
For it is all in season.

Note: This is an ode used at district entertainments. The domain of the king was divided into six districts, of which the more trusted and able officers were presented every third year to the king and feasted. The same took place in the States which were divided into three districts. At the former of those entertainments, this ode was sung first. Lines 1 and 3 of the first three stanzas were sung by one guest and the other lines by all the guests in chorus.

(17) SECOND DECADE OF ODES

171. A Drinking Song

Southern fish fine
  Swim to and fro.
Our host has wine;
  Guests drink and glow.

Southern fish fine
  Swim all so free.
Our host has wine;
  Guests drink with glee.

South wood is fine
  And gourds are sweet.
Our host has wine;
  With cheer guests meet.

Birds fly in line
  O'er dale and hill.
Our host has wine;
  Guests drink their fill.

Note: This is a festal ode appropriate to the entertainment of worthy guests,
who are compared to gourds in the 3rd stanza and birds in the 4th. It celebrates the general sympathy of the entertainer compared to the wood.

172. Longevity

Plants on south hill
  And northern grass.
Enjoy your fill,
  Men of first class!

Second Decade of Odes 179

May you live long
Among the throng!

South mulberries,
  North poplars straight.
Enjoy if you please,
  Men of the State!
May you live long
Among the throng!

Plums on south hill,
  North medlar trees.
Enjoy your fill,
  Lord, as you please!
You're people's friend;
Your fame has no end.

Plant on south hill
  And northern tree.
Enjoy your fill
  Of longevity!
You're a good mate
Of our good State.

Trees on south hill
  And north, all told,
Enjoy your fill
  And live till old!
O may felicity
Fall to posterity!

Note: This is a festal ode where the host, the ruler, celebrates the virtues of his ministers, the guests, proclaims his complacency in them and supplicates blessings on them.

173. A Festal Song

How long grows the southernwood
  With dew on it so bright!
Now I see my men good,
  My heart is glad and light.
We talk and laugh and feast;
Of our care we are eased.

How high grows the southernwood
  With heavy dew so bright!
Now we see our lord good
  Like dragon and sunlight.
With impartiality
He'll enjoy longevity.

How green grows the southernwood
  Wet with fallen dew bright!
Now I see my men good.
  Let us feast with delight
And enjoy brotherhood!
  Be happy day and night!

How sweet the southernwood
  In heavy dew does stand!
Now we see our lord good
  Holding the reins in hand.
Bells ringing far and near,
We're happy without peer.

Note: This is an ode sung on the occasion of the king's entertaining the feudal princes who had come to his court. The host is the speaker in the first and third stanzas and the guests in the second and the last.

174. A Festive Song

The heavy dew so bright
   Is dried up on the trunk.
Feasting long all the night,
   None will retire till drunk.

The heavy dew is bright
   On lush grass in the dell.
We feast long all the night
   Till rings the temple bell.

Bright is the heavy dew
   On date and willow trees.
Our noble guests are true
   And good at perfect ease.

The plane and jujube trees
   Have their fruits hanging down.
Our noble guests will please
   In manner and renown.

Note: This is an ode proper to the convivial entertainment of the feudal
princes at the royal court.

175. The Red Bow

Receive the red bow unbent
   And have it stored,
It's a gift I present
   To a guest adored.
Hear drum and bell
And let's feast well!

Receive the red bow unbent
  Fitt'd on its frame,
It's a gift I present
  To a guest of fame.
Hear drum and bell
And let's drink well!

Receive the red bow unbent
  Placed in its case,
It's a gift I present
  To a guest with grace.
Hear bell and drum;
Let's drink welcome!

Note: This is a festal ode sung on the occasion of a feast given by the king
to a prince on recognition of the merit he had achieved. The conferring of a
red bow was the highest testimonial of merit, for red was the color of honor
in the Zhou dynasty.

176. Our Good Lord

Lush, lush grows southernwood
  In the midst of the heights.
Now we see our lord good,
  We greet him with delight.

Lush, lush grows southernwood
  In the midst of the isle.
Now we see our lord good,
  Our faces beam with smiles.

Lush, lush grows southernwood
  In the midst of the hills.
Now we see our lord good,
  He gives us shells at will.

The boat of willow wood
    Sinks or swims east or west.
Now we see our lord good,
    Our hearts can be at rest.

Note: This ode celebrates the attention paid to education by the king
inspecting the schools of the State, who, having provided for the training of
the talents, saw also to their being thereafter furnished with offices and
salary. Up to the time of the Qin dynasty shells were current as money
in China. The last stanza is metaphorical of the talented youth of the
kingdom, without aim or means of culture, until they were cared for by
the king.

177. General Ji Fu

Days in sixth moon are long,
    Chariots ready to fight.
All of our horses are strong,
    Flags and banners in flight.
The Huns come in a wild band;
    Danger's imminent.
To save our royal land
    An expedition's sent.

My four black steeds are strong,
    Trained with skill and address.
Days in sixth moon are long,
    We've made our battle dress.
Nice battle dress is made;
    Each day thirty li done.
Our forces make a raid,
    Ordered by Heaven's Son.

My four steeds are strong ones,
    With their heads in harness.

We fight against the Huns
In view of great success.
Careful and strict we'd be;
In battle dress we stand.
In battle dress stand we
To defend the king's land.

The Huns cross the frontier;
Our riverside towns fall.
The invaders come near
North of our capital.
Like flying birds we speed,
With silken flags aglow.
Ten large war chariots lead
The way against the foe.

The chariots move along
And proceed high and low.
The four horses are strong
And at high speed they go.
We fight against the Huns
As far as the northern border.
Wise Ji Fu leads brave sons
And puts the state in order.

Ji Fu feasts his friends here
With his gifts on display.
He's back from the frontier,
Having come a long way.
He entertains his friends
With roast turtles and fish.
The filial Zhang Zhong spends
His time there by Ji's wish.

Note: This ode and the thirteen which follow all refer to the time of King
Xuan (826—781 BC), who despatched General Ji Fu against the Hunnish

invaders. The writer of this ode is Zhang Zhong, whose name is mentioned
in the last stanza.

178. General Fang

Let's gather millet white
   In newly broken land!
General Fang will alight
   Here to take the command.
Three thousand cars arrive
   With his great well – trained forces.
The general takes a drive
   On four black and white horses.
Four piebalds in a row
   Draw chariot red and green,
With reins and hooks aglow,
   Seal skin and bamboo screen.

Let's gather millet white
   In newly broken land!
General Fang will alight
   On the field rein in hand.
Three thousand cars arrive
   With flags and banners spread.
The general leads the drive
   In chariot painted red.
Hear eight bells tinkling sound
   And gems of pendant ring.
See the golden girdle round
   His robe conferred by the king!

Rapid is the hawks' flight:
   They soar up to the sky
And then here they alight.

General Fang comes nigh;
Three thousand cars arrive;
    His well-trained soldiers come.
General Fang leads the drive;
    Men jingle and beat drums.
His forces in array,
    The general has good fame,
Drums rolling on display,
    And flags streaming in flame.

You southern savage dare
    To invade our great land.
Our General Fang is there;
    At war he's a good hand.
The general leads his forces,
    To make captives of the crowd.
His chariot drawn by horses
    Now rumbles now rolls loud
Like clap or roll of thunder.
    General Fang in command
Puts the Huns down and under
    And southern savage band.

Note: This ode celebrates General Fang who had been one of the leaders in
the northern expedition under General Ji Fu (See ode 177) and who con-
ducted this grand southern expedition in 825 BC.

179. Great Hunting

Our chariots strong
    Have well-matched steeds.
Our train is long;
    Eastward it speeds.

Our chariots good,
  Four steeds in front,
Drive to the east wood
  Where we shall hunt.

Our lord afield,
  Flags on display,
With archers skilled
  Pursues his prey.

He drives four steeds
  Strong and aglow.
Red-shoed, he leads
  His men in a row.

Strings fit, we choose
  Arrows and bows.
Archers in twos
  Reap games in rows.

Four yellow steeds
  Run straight and fit.
Our chariot speeds,
  Each shot a hit.

Long, long steeds neigh;
  Flags float and stream.
Footmen look gay;
  With smiles cooks beam.

On backward way
  We hear no noise.
What happy day!
  How we rejoice!

Note: This ode celebrates a great hunt presided over by King Xuan on the occasion of his giving audience to the feudal princes at the eastern capital of Luo after two military victories, one won by General Ji Fu over the northern tribes in 826 BC, and another by General Fang over the southern tribes in 825 BC (See odes 177 and 178).

180. Royal Hunting

On a lucky vernal day
  We pray to Steed Divine.
Our chariot strong and fine, in array
  Four horses stand in line.
We come to wooded height
And chase the herds in flight.
Three days after we pray,
  Our chosen steeds appear.
We chase all kinds of prey:
  Roebucks, does, stags and deer.
We come to riverside
Where Heaven's Son may ride.

Look to the plain we choose:
  There are all kinds of prey,
Here in threes, there in twos,
  Now they rush, now they stay.
We chase from left and right
To the royal delight.
See the king bend his bow,
  Put arrows on the string,
On a boar let it go;
  A rhino's killed by the king.
He invites guests to dine
With cups brimful of wine.

Note: This ode celebrates a hunting expedition by King Xuan on a smaller scale, attended by his own officers and within the royal domain.

(18) THIRD DECADE OF ODES

181. The Toilers

Wild geese fly high
  With wings a-rustling.
We toilers hie
  Afield a-bustling.
Some mourn their fate:
They've lost their mate.

Wild geese in flight
In marsh alight.
We build the wall
From spring to fall.
We've done our best,
But have no rest.

Wild geese fly high;
They mourn and cry.
The wise may know
  Our toil and pain.
The fool says, "No,
  Do not complain!"

Note: The geese seeking rest and finding none, are introduced as illustrative
of the condition in which the people found themselves, scattered about with
no house to live in and building walls of earth and lime from spring to autumn without rest.

182. Early Audience

How goes the night?
It's at its height.
In royal court a hundred torches blaze bright.
Before my lords appear,
Their ringing bells I'll hear.

How goes the night?
It's passed its height.
In royal court the torches shed a lambent light.
Before my lords appear,
Their tinkling bells will come near.

How goes the night?
Morning is near.
In royal court is blown out torches' light.
Now all my lords appear,
I see their banners from here.

Note: This is a soliloquy of King Xuan, waking now and again in his anxiety not to be late for his morning levee. The great torch of 100 faggots
bound together is kept burning all night inside the entrance gate leading to
the assembly hall, where the king will be ready to receive the princes and nobles at early dawn. He awakes again and again and judges of the time from
what was or what he fancied must be, the state of the great torch.

183. To Friends

The waters flow
    Towards the ocean.
Hawks fly in slow
    Or rapid motion.
My friends and brothers,
    Alas! don't care

For their fathers and mothers
  Nor State affairs.

The waters flow
  In current strong.
Hawks fly now low
  Now high and long.
None play their part
  But hatch their plot.
What breaks my heart
  Can't be forgot.

The waters flow
  At rising tide.
Hawks fly so low
  Along hillside.
Let's put an end
  To talks ill bred,
Respectful friend,
  Lest slanders spread!

Note: This ode bewails the disorder of the times and a general indifference to it, and traces the problem to the slanderers encouraged by the conduct of men in power. The first two lines of the last stanza, missing in the original, are supplanted by the translator.

184. A Garden State

In the marsh the crane cries;
  Her voice is heard for miles.
Hid in the deep a fish lies
  Or it swims by the isles.
Pleasant a garden's made
  By sandal trees standing still
And small trees in their shade.

Stones from another hill
May be used to polish jade.

In the marsh the crane cries;
    Her voice is heard on high.
By the isle the fish lies
    Or in the deep near-by.
Pleasant the garden in our eyes
    Where sandal trees stand still
And paper mulberries 'neath them.
    Stones from another hill
May be used to polish gem.

Note: The garden described in this ode alludes to a State, the crane and sandal trees to manifested talents, the fish, small trees and paper mulberries to undiscovered talents, and stones from another hill to unpolished talents from other States. It is important for a State to discover and employ different talents.

185. The Minister of War

O minister of war!
    We're soldiers of the crown.
Why send us to an expeditionary corps
    So that we cannot settle down?

O minister of war!
    We're guardians of the land.
Why send us to an expeditionary corps
    So that we're under endless command?

O minister of war!
    Why don't you listen to others?
Why send us to an expeditionary corps
    So that we cannot feed our mothers?

Note: The soldiers of the Royal Guard complain of the service imposed on
them by the Minister of War in 787 BC, when the royal army had sustained
a great defeat from some of the northern tribes and the royal guards were ordered to join the force for the north, a duty which did not belong to them

186. To a Guest

The pony white
    Feeds on the hay.
Tether it tight;
    Lengthen the joy of the day
So that its owner may
At ease here stay.

The pony white
    Feeds on bean leaves.
Tether it tight;
    Lengthen the joy of the eves
So that its owner may
As guest here stay.

The pony so white
    Brings pleasure here.
My guest so bright,
    Be in good cheer!
Enjoy at ease!
Don't take leave, please!

The pony so white
    Feeds on fresh grass.
My guest gem-bright
    Leaves me, alas!
O from you let me hear
So that to me you're near!

Note: The detaining of the pony shows how the writer longs to have its master always with him. In the last stanza the writer expresses his regret at the guest's departure, and still hopes that he will retain some connection with himself.

187. I Will Go Back

O yellow birds, hear please!
Don't settle on the trees!
Don't eat my paddy grain!
The people here won't deign
To treat foreigners well.
I will go back and dwell
In my family cell.

O yellow birds, hear please!
Don't perch on mulberries!
Don't eat my sorghum grain!
The people here won't deign
Strangers to understand.
I will go back offhand
To my dear brethren's land.

O yellow birds, hear please!
Don't settle on oat-trees!
Don't eat my millet grain!
The people here won't deign
To let me live at ease.
So I'll go back again
To my dear uncles' plain.

Note: Some officer, who had withdrawn to another State, finds his expectations of the people there disappointed, and proposes to return to the royal domain.

188. A Rejected Husband

I go by countryside
  With withered trees o'erspread.
With you I would reside
  For to you I was wed.
Now you reject my hand,
I'll go back to my land.

I go by countryside
  With sheep's foot overspread.
I'd sleep by your bedside
  For to you I was wed.
Now you reject my hand,
I'll go back to homeland.

I go by countryside
  With pokeweed overspread.
You drove husband outside,
  To another you'll wed.
I can't bear your disdain,
So I go back with pain.

Note: This is the first ode in the *Book of Songs*, of a rejected husband complaining of his wife.

189. Installation

The brook so clean,
  Mountains so long,
Bamboo so green,
  Lush pines so strong.
O brothers dear,
  Do love each other!

Make no scheme here
    Against your brother!

Inherit all
    From father's tombs.
Build solid wall
    And hundred rooms,
With doors southwest
    Where you may walk
And sit or rest
    And laugh or talk.

The frames well bound
For earth they pound,
No wind nor rain,
    No bird nor mouse
Could spoil in vain
    Your noble house.

As man stands right,
    As arrow's straight,
As birds in flight
    Spread wings so great,
'Tis the abode
Fit for our lord.

Square is the hall
With pillars tall.
The chamber's bright,
    The bedroom's deep.
Our lord at night
    May rest and sleep.

Bamboo outspread
On rush-mat bed

Where you may rest
    Or lie awake
Or have dreams blest
    Of bear or snake.

Witches divine
The bear's a sign
Of newborn son
And the snake's one
Of daughter fine.

When a son's blest,
    In bed he's laid,
In robe he's drest,
    And plays with jade.
His cry is loud,
Of crown he's proud,
He'll lord o'er the crowd.

When a daughter's blest,
    She's put aground,
In wrappers drest,
    She'll play with spindle round.
She'd do nor wrong nor good
But care for wine and food;
She'd cause her parents dear
No woe nor fear.

Note: This ode was probably made for a festival on the completion and dedi-
cation of a palace, of which there is a description with good wishes for the
builder and his posterity. The first four lines of Stanza 1 are descriptive of
the situation of the palace and the last four lines are a prayer that it might
be the abode of concord and harmony. Stanzas 2 and 3 describe mainly the
process of the building; stanzas 4 and 5 describe the king's abode and his
bedroom. In stanza 6 we have the king sleeping and dreaming and in stanza
7 the witch interpreting his dream. The last two stanzas show clearly the different estimation in which boys and girls were held in ancient China.

190. The Herdsmen's Song

Who says you have no sheep?
  There're three hundred in the herd.
Have you no cows to keep?
  Ninety cattle's lows are heard.
Your sheep don't strive for corn;
They're at pace horn to horn.
When your cattle appear,
You see their flapping ears.

Some cattle go downhill;
  Others drink water clear.
Some move; others lie still.
  When your herdsmen appear,
They bear hats of bamboo
  And carry food and rice.
Cattle of thirty hues
  Are fit for sacrifice.

Then come your men of the herds
  With large and small firewood,
And male and female birds.
  Your sheep appear so good:
Fat, they don't run away;
Tame, they don't go astray.
At a wave of arms, behold!
They come back to the fold.

Then dreams the man of herds
  Of locusts turned to fishes,
Tortoise and snake to birds.
  The witch divines our wishes:

The locust turned to fish
 Foretells a bumper year;
The snakes turned, as we wish,
 To greater household with cheer.

Note: The sheep do not butt one another with their horns and the cattle flap their ears: these are indicative of harmony and health. Sacrifice is specified merely as one of the various uses for which sheep and cattle served. The herdsman's dream gives the idea of increasing numbers. This ode celebrates the largeness and condition of King Xuan's flocks and herds under the auspices of the prosperous of the Kingdom.

(19) FOURTH DECADE OF ODES

191. To Grand Master Yin

South Mountain's high;
    Crags and jags tower.
Our people's eye
    Looks to your power.
We're in distress
    For state affairs
Are in a mess.
    Why don't you care?

South Mountain's high,
    Rugged here and there.
In people's eye
    You're as unfair.
Distress and woes
    Fall without end.
Our grievance grows,
    But you won't mend.

Master Yin stands
    Pillar of State.
With power in hands
    You rule our fate.
On you rely
    People and crown.
Heaven on high!
    You've false renown.

Is what you do
    Worthy of trust?

We don't think you
   Have used men just.
You put the mean
   In a high place.
Let all your kin
   Fall in disgrace!

Heaven unfair
   And pitiless
Sends man to scare;
   We're in distress.
Send us men just
   To bring us rest;
Send men we trust;
   We are not distressed.

Great Heaven, oh!
   Troubles ne'er cease.
Each month they grow
   And we've no peace.
We're grieved at heart.
   Who rule and reign,
State set apart?
   We toil with pain.

I drive my four
   Steeds in harness.
I look before
   And see distress.

On evil day
   You wield your spears.
When you are gay,
·   You drink with cheers.

Heaven's unjust;
    Our king's no rest.
To our disgust
    Alone you're blest.

I sing to lay
    Evil deeds bare
So that you may
    Mind state affairs.

Note: This is a lament over the miserable state of the kingdom, denouncing
the injustice and carelessness of the Grand-Master Yin as the cause of it,
and blaming also the conduct of King You, who reigned 780−770 BC, and
after whose death there took place the removal of royal residence to the eastern capital — the great event in the history of the Zhou dynasty.

192. Lamentation

In frosty moon
    My heart is grieved.
Rumors spread soon
    Can't be believed.
I stand alone;
    My grief won't go.
With cares I groan
    And ill I grow.

Why wasn't I born
    Before or after?
I suffer scorn
    From people's laughter.
Good words or bad
    Are what they say.
My heart feels sad,
    Filled with dismay.

My heart feels grieved;
  Unlucky am I.
People deceived,
  Slaves and maids cry.
Alas for me!
  Can I be blest?
The crow I see,
  Where can it rest?

See in the wood
  Branch large or small.
For livelihood
  We suffer all.
Dark is the sky.
  Who'll make it clear?
Heavens on high
  Cause hate and fear.

The hills said low
  Are mountains high.
Why don't we go
  Against the lie?
About our dream,
  What do they know?
Though wise they seem,
  They can't tell male
From female crow.
  To what avail?

High are the skies;
  Down I must bow.
Thick the earth lies;
  I must walk slow.
Though what I say
  Has no mistakes,

Men of today
  Bite me like snakes.

See rugged fields
  Where lush grows grain.
How can I yield
  To might and main?
I was sought after
  But couldn't be got.
With pride and laughter
  They use me not.

Laden with cares,
  My heart seems bound.
The state affairs
  In woe are drowned.
The flames though high
  May be put out.
The world's lost by
  Fair Lady Bao.

Long grieved my heart,
  I meet hard rain.
Loaded your cart,
  No wheels remain.
O'erturned 'twill lie;
  For help you'd cry.

Keep your wheel-aid
And spoke well-made.
Show oft concern
  For driver good
Lest he o'erturn
  Your cart of wood.
You may get o'er

Difficulties,
But not before
You've thought of this.

Fish in the pool
Knows no delight.
Deep in water cool
They're still in sight.
Saddened, I hate
Evils of the state.

They have wine sweet
And viands good,
So they can treat
Their neighborhood.
In loneliness
I feel distress.

The poor have houses small;
Their food is coarse.
Woes on them fall;
They've no resource.
Happy the rich class;
But the poor, alas!

Note: This is a lament over the miseries of the kingdom and the ruin
coming on it, all through King You's employment of worthless men and his
indulgence of his favorite Lady Bao Shi.

193. President Huang Fu

In the tenth month the sun and moon
Cross each other on the first day.
The sun was then eclipsed at noon,
An evil omen, people say.

The moon became then small,
    The sun became not bright.
The people one and all
    Are in a wretched plight.

Bad omen, moon and sun
    Don't keep their proper way.
In the state evil's done;
    The good are kept away.
The eclipse of the moon
    Is not uncommon thing;
That of the sun at noon
    Will dire disaster bring.

Lightning flashes, rolls thunder,
    There is no peace nor rest.
The streams bubble from under;
    Crags fall from mountain-crest.
The heights become deep vale;
    Deep vales turn into height.
Men of this time bewail:
    What to do with such plight?

Huang Fu presides o'er the state;
    Fan the interior.
Jia Bo is magistrate;
    Zhong Yong is minister.
Of worthy deeds Zou keeps record;
    Of stable Kui takes care.
Yu is a noble lord;
    All flatter Lady Bao the fair.

Oh, this Huang Fu would say
    He's done all by decree,
But why drive me away

Without consulting me?
Why move my house along
    And devastate my land?
Has he done nothing wrong?
    The law is in his hand.

Huang Fu says he is wise
    And builds the capital.
He chooses men we despise,
    Corrupt and greedy all.
No men of worthy deeds
    Are left to guard the crown;
Those who have cars and steeds
    Can reside in the town.

I work hard all day long;
    Of my toil I'm not proud.
I have done nothing wrong;
    Against me slander's loud.
Distress of any kind
    Does not come from on high.
Good words or bad behind
    Would raise a hue and cry.

My homeland far away,
    I feel so sad and drear.
Other people are gay;
    Alone I am grieved here.
When all people are free,
    Why can't I take my ease?
I dread Heaven's decree;
    I can't as my friends do what I please.

Note: In this ode an officer laments the signs, celestial and terrestial, betokening the ruin of Zhou. He expounds the true causes of these and names Huang Fu and other chief culprits.

194. A Loyal Officer

The heaven high,
   Unkind for long,
Spreads far and nigh
   Famine on throng.
Heaven unfair,
You have no care
   Nor have you thought.
Sinners are freed;
   Those who sin not,
Why should they bleed?

Will you see the fall
Of Zhou capital?
Ministers gone,
   None knows my toil
Nor serves the throne
   But all recoil.
Of the lords none
   At court appear.
No good is done
   But evil mere.

Why isn't just word
Believed when heard?
Travelers know
Nowhere to go.
O lords, be good
And show manhood!
Don't you revere
Heaven you fear?

After the war
Famine's not o'er.

I, a mere groom,
Am full of gloom.
Among lords who
Will speak the true?
They like good words;
Bad ones aren't heard.

Alas! what's true
    Cannot be said,
Or woe on you,
    Your tongue and head.
If you speak well
    Like stream ne'er dry,
You will excel
    And soon rise high.

It's hard to be
    An officer.
The wrongs you see
    Make you incur
Displeasure great
    Of Heaven's Son,
Or in the state
    Friends you have none.

Go back to the capital!
    You say your home's not there.
My bitter tears would fall
    To say what you can't bear:
"When you left, who
Built a house for your?"

Note: A groom of the chambers mourns over the miserable state of the kingdom, the incorrigible course of the king and the retirement from office and re-
sponsibility of many lords. Lines 7 and 8 of the second stanza are illustrated
by the fact that the loss of the capital and the death of King You in 770

BC were at last owing to the refusal of the princes to come to his aid. They had once been deceived by the cry of "wolf," and when the wolf really came, they remained in their own States, thinking the alarm was false. Lines 9 and 10 express the folly and madness of King You, who cried wolf so that all the princes came to his rescue, only to provoke laughter of his favorite Lady Bao Shi. In the last stanza the writer still appeals to all officers of worth who had withdrawn from the capital, urges them to resume their duties and shows the inconsistency of the reason they alleged for not doing so.

195. Counsellors

The Heaven's ire
  On earth descends.
The counsels dire
  Go without ends.
They follow one
  Not good but bad.
The good not done,
  I feel so sad.

Controversy
  Is to be rued.
They disagree
  On what is good.
On what is bad
  They will depend.
I feel not glad:
  How will this end?

The tortoise bored,
  Nothing's foretold.
Men on the board
  No right uphold.
The more they say;
  The less they do.

They won't start on their way.
    How can we ask them to?

Alas! formers of plan
    Won't follow those of yore.
No principles they can
    Formulate as before.
They follow counselors
    Who can nothing good yield.
They talk to wayfarers
    About houses to build.

Though bounded is our state,
    Our men may be wise or not.
Our numbers are not great;
    They know to plan and plot.
They are able to think
    Like stream from spring will flow.
Together they will sink
    In common weal and woe.

Don't fight a tiger with bare hand,
    Nor cross without a boat the stream.
You may know one thing in your land,
    But not two as you deem.
Be careful as if you did stand
    On the brink of the gulf of vice
    Or tread upon thin ice!

Note: This is a lament over the recklessness and incapacity of King You's
plans and of his counsellors. Lines 7 and 8 of the 4th stanza may be illustrated as follows: if a man wishes to travel, he must ask those who have
travelled the road. If he consult with men who have not travelled it, it is rea-
sonable he should learn nothing about it.

196. Reflections

Small is the cooing dove,
But it can fly above.
My heart feels sad and drear,
Missing my parents dear.
Till daybreak I can't sleep,
Lost so long in thoughts deep.

Those who are grave and wise,
    When they drink, won't get drunk;
But those who have dull eyes
    In drinking will be sunk.
From drinking be restrained!
What's lost can't be regained.

There are beans in the plain;
People gather their grain.
The insect has young ones;
    The sphex bears them away.
So teach and train your sons
    Lest they should go astray!

The wagtails wing their ways
    And twittering, they're gone.
Advancing are my days;
    Your months are going on.
Early to rise and late to bed!
Don't disgrace those by whom you're bred!

The greenbeaks on their tour
    Peck grain in the stack-yard.
I am lonely and poor,
    Unfit for working hard.

I go out to divine
How can I not decline

Precarious, ill at ease,
As if perched on trees;
Careful lest I should ail
On the brink of a vale;
I tremble twice or thrice
As if treading on thin ice.

Note: Some officer, at a time of disorder and misgovernment, urges on his brother the duty of maintaining his own virtue and of observing great caution.

197. The Banished

With flapping wings the crows
Come back, flying in rows.
All people gay appear;
Alone I'm sad and drear.
What crime and sin have I
Committed against the sky?
With pain my heart's pierced through.
Alas! what can I do?

The highway should be plain,
    But it's o'ergrown with grass.
My heart is wound'd with pain
    As if I'm pound'd, alas!
Sighing, I lie still dressed;
    My grief makes me grow old.
I feel deeply distressed,
    Gnawed by headache untold.

The mulberry and other
Trees planted by our mother
And father are protected
As our parents respected.
Without the fur outside
And the lining inside,
Can we live at a time
Without reason or rhyme?

Lush grow the willow trees;
Cicadas trill at ease.
In water deep and clear
Rushes and reeds appear.
Adrift I'm like a boat;
I know not where I float.
My heart deeply distressed,
In haste I lie down dressed.

Off the stag goes
    At a fast gait;
The pheasant crows,
    Seeking his mate.
The ruined tree
    Stripped of its leaves
Has saddened me.
    Who knows what grieves?

The captured hare
    May be released;
The dead o'er there
    Buried at least.
The prince can't bear
    The sight of me;
Laden with care,
    My tears flow free.

Slanders believed
  As a toast drunk,
The king's deceived,
  In thoughts not sunk.
The branch cut down,
  They leave the tree.
The guilty let alone,
  They impute guilt to me.

Though higher than a mountain
And deeper than a fountain,
The king ne'er speaks light word or jeers,
For even walls have ears.
  "Do not approach my dam,
  Nor move my net away!
Rejected as I am,
  What more have I to say?"

Note: The eldest son and heir-apparent of King You bewails his banishment, as the king, enamoured of Lady Bao Shi and led away by slanderers, announced that a child by that lady should be his successor. The last four lines are quotations from song 35 "A Rejected Wife". The writer must have been familiar with that song and these lines suited both his circumstances and purpose.

198. Disorder and Slander

O great Heaven on high,
  You're called our parent dear.
Why make the guiltless cry
  And spread turmoil far and near?
You cause our terror great;
  We're worried for the guiltless.
You rule our hapless fate;
  We're worried in distress.

Sad disorder comes then
    When untruth is received.
Disorder comes again
    When slanders are believed.
If we but blame falsehood,
    Disorder will decrease.
If we but praise the good,
    Disorder soon will cease.

If we make frequent vows,
    Disorder will still grow.
If we to thieves make bows,
    They will bring greater woe.
What they say may be sweet;
    The woe grows none the less.
The disorder complete
    Will cause the king's distress.

The temple's grand,
    Erected for ages.
Great work is planned
    By kings and sages.
Judge others' mind
    But by our own!
The hound can find
    Hares running down.

The supple tree
    Planted by the good.
From slander free,
    You can tell truth from falsehood.
Grandiose word
Should not be heard.
Sweet sounding one
    Like organ-tongue

Can deceive none
   Except the young.

Who is that knave
   On river's border,
Not strong nor brave,
   Root of disorder?
You look uncanny.
   How bold are you?
Your plans seem many;
   Your followers are few.

Note: The writer, suffering because of slanderous remarks to the king, appeals to Heaven, dwells on the nature and evil of slander and expresses his hatred and contempt for the slanderers.

199. A Fair-Weather Friend

Who's the man coming here
   So deep and full of hate?
My dam he's coming near,
   But enters not my gate.
Is he a follower
Of the tyrant? Yes, sir.

Two friends we did appear;
   Alone I am in woes.
My dam he's coming near,
   But past my gate he goes.
He is different now,
For he's broken his vow.

Who's the man coming here
   Passing before my door?

His voice I only hear,
But see no man of yore.
How can he not fear then
Neither heaven nor men?

Who's the man coming forth
Like a whirlwind which roars?
Why does he not go north
Nor to the southern shores?
Why comes he near my dam
And disturbs what I am?

Even when you walk slow,
You won't stop where you are,
And then when fast you go,
How can you grease your car?
You will not come to see
Nor will you comfort me.

If you should but come in,
Then I would feel at ease.
But you do not come in,
I know you're hard to please.
You will not come to see
Nor will set my heart free.

Earthern whistle you blew;
I played bamboo flute long.
When I was friend with you,
We had sung the same song.
Before offerings now,
How can you forget your vow?

I curse you as a ghost,
For you have left no trace.

I will not be your host:
    I see your ugly face.
But I sing in distress
For you are pitiless.

Note; The writer, suffering from slander and suspecting that the slanderer
was an old friend, intimates the grounds of his suspicion and laments his
case, while welcoming the restoration of their former relations.

200. A Eunuch's Song to Slanderers

A few lines made to be
Fair shell-embroidery,
You slanderers in dress
Have gone to great excess.

The Sieve stars in the south
Opening wide their mouth,
You vile slanderers, who
Devise the schemes for you?

You talk so much, so well;
In slander you excel.
Take care of what you say.
Will you be believed? Nay.

You may think you are clever,
Slandering people ever.
They may be deceived, but learn
That you'll be punished in turn!

The proud are in delight,
The crowd in sorry plight.
Heaven bright, heaven bright!

Look on the proud;
Pity the crowd!

Oh, you vile slanderers,
Who are your counselors?
I would throw you to feed
The wolf's or tiger's greed.
If they refuse to eat,
I'd tread you down my feet
Or cast you to north land.
Or throw you to Heaven's hand.

The eunuch Mengzi, I
Go to the Garden High
By a willowy road long
And make this plaintive song.
Officials on your way,
Hearken to it, I pray!

Note: A eunuch, suffering from slander, complains of his fate and warns and
denounces his enemies. It is assumed that his own mutilation was in consequence of the slanders from which he had suffered. The shell-embroidery in
the first stanza is a piece of silk embroidered till it looks like a beautiful
shell. By the combination of a few lines a striking effect may be produced,
and so had it been when some trivial faults of the writer had been magnified
and woven, as it were, by his slanderers, into great crimes. The Sieve in the
second stanza is the name of one of the 28 constellations of the zodiac. It
consists of four stars, two which are called "the Heels," close together,
and two, more widely apart, which are called "the Mouth." The Sieve
stars open their mouth wide as the slanderer.

(20) FIFTH DECADE OF ODES

201. A Castoff Woman

Strong winds hard blow,
   Followed by rain.
In times of woe
   Firm we'd remain;
Cast off in weal,
Lonely I feel.

Strong winds hard blow,
   From morn till night.
In times of woe
   You held me tight;
Cast off in weal,
How sad I feel!

Strong winds blow high,
   But mountains stand.
No grass but dies,
   Nor trees in land.
Much good's forgot;
Small faults are not.

Note: A castoff woman complains of the rejection of her husband, caused by
his improved circumstances.

202. Death of Parents

Long and large grows the sweet grass,
   Not wild weed of no worth.

My parents dear, alas!
   With toil you gave me birth.

Long and large grows the sweet grass,
   Not shorter weed on earth.
My parents dear, alas!
   With pain you gave me birth.

When the pitcher is void,
   Empty will be the jar.
Our parents' life destroyed,
   How sad we orphans are!
Fatherless, on whom to rely?
   Motherless, on whom to depend?
Abroad, with grief I sigh:
   At home, whom may I tend?

My father gave me birth;
   By mother I was fed.
They cherished me with mirth,
   And by them I was bred.
They looked after me
   And bore me out and in.
Boundless as sky should be
   The kindness of our kin.

The southern mountain's high,
   The wind soughs without cheer.
Happy are those near-by;
   Alone I'm sad and drear.

The southern mountain's cold;
   The wind blows a strong blast.
Happy are young and old;
   My grief fore'er will last.

Note: A son deplores his hard fate in being prevented from rendering the last services to his parents and enlarges on the parental claim. The sweet grass is much superior to the weed. The writer feels that by the discharge of his duty to his parents to the last, he should have proved himself like a sweet grass, whereas, having failed in that duty, he was only like the weed.

203. Inequality

The tripod's full of food;
They eat with spoons of wood.
The road's smooth like whetstone
For lords to go alone.
Like arrow it is straight,
On which no people circulate.
Recalling bygone years,
In streams run down my tears.

In East states, large and small,
The looms are empty all.
In summer shoes we go
On winter frost or snow.
Even the noble sons
Walk on foot like poor ones.
Seeing them come and go,
My heart is full of woe.

Cold water passing by,
　Do not soak our firewood!
Woeful we wake and sigh
　For scanty livelihood.
If our firewood is dry,
　We may carry it west.
If wet, we can but sigh.
　Oh! when may we have rest?

We toilers of the East
    Are not paid as those of the West;
The Western nobles at least
    Are all splendidly drest.
The rich and noble sons
    Don't care about their furs,
But as slaves the poor ones
    Serve all the officers.

If we present them wine,
They do not think it fine.
If we present them jade,
They don't think it well-made.
The Silver River bright
Looks down on us in light.
The weaving Stars are three;
All day long they're not free.

Though all day long they move,
They weave nothing above.
Bright is the Cowherd Star,
But it won't draw our car.
Morning Star in the east,
    Evening Star in the west,
Eight Net Stars catch no beast.
    What use though they don't rest?

In south the Winnowing Fan
Cannot sift grain for man.
In north the Dipper fine
Cannot ladle good wine.
The Sieve shines in the south,
Idly showing its mouth.
In the north shines the Plough
With handle like a bow.

Note: An officer of one of the eastern States ruled by the descendants of the Shang dynasty deplores the exactions made from them by the Zhou government, complains of the favor shown to the west, contrasts the misery of the present with the happiness of the past and vents his indignation by claiming there is deceit even in Heaven where stars do not live up to their fine names: The Winnowing Fan cannot winnow and the Dipper cannot hold wine.

204. Banishment

From fourth to sixth moon when
   The summer heat remains,
Our fathers are kind men.
   Can they leave me in pain?

The autumn days are chill;
   All plants and grass decay.
In distress I am ill.
   Where can I go? Which way?

In winter days severe
   The vehement wind blows.
No one feels sad and drear.
   Why am I alone in woes?

Trees on the hill were good,
   And mume trees far and nigh.
Who has destroyed the wood?
   Who knows the reason why?

Water from the fountain flows
   Now muddy and now clear.
But I'm each day in woes.
   How can I not be drear?

The rivers east and west
   Crisscross in southern land.
In work I did my best.
   Who'd give me helping hand?

Like hawk or eagle why
   Cannot I skyward go?
Like fish why cannot I
   Go to hide down below?

Above grow fern in the throng,
   And medlars spread below.
Alas! I've made this song

   To ease my heart of woe.

Note: A banished officer deplores the misery he has suffered in summer, autumn and winter, compares himself to destroyed trees and muddy water, and complains that he is not so free as hawk and fish, and that he cannot grow like ferns and medlars.

205. Injustice

To gather medlars long,
   I go up northern height.
All the officers strong
   Are busy day and night
For the royal affairs.
Who for our parents cares?

The land under the sky
   Is all the king's domain;
The people far and nigh
   Are under royal reign.
But ministers unfair
Load me with heavy care.

Four steeds run without rest
　For state affairs all day long.
They say I'm at my best
　And few like me are strong.
I have a robust chest
And may go east and west.

Some enjoy rest and ease;
　Some worn out for the state.
Some march on without cease;
　Some lie in bed early and late.

Some know not people's pain;
　Some toil for state affairs.
Some long in bed remain;
　Some laden with great cares.

Some drink all the day long;
　Others worry for woe.
Some only say all's wrong;
　To hard work others go.

Note: An officer complains of the arduous and continual duties unequally imposed upon him, keeping him away from his duty to his parents, while others are left to enjoy their ease.

206. Don't Trouble

Don't push an ox-drawn cart
　Or you'll raise dust about.
Do not trouble your heart
　Or you'll be ill, no doubt.

Don't push an ox-drawn cart
  Or dust will dim your sight.
Do not trouble your heart
  Or you can't see the light.

Don't push an ox-drawn cart
  Or dust will darken the way.
Do not trouble your heart
  Or you will pine away.

Note: This ode reads like the song of a driver who advises people not to do anything beyond human power lest it should get them into trouble.

207. A Nostalgic Official

O Heaven high and bright,
On lower world shed light!
Westward I came by order
As far as this wild border,
Of second month then on first day;
Now cold and heat have passed away.
Alas! my heart is sad
As poison drives me mad.
I think of those in power;
My tears fall down in showers.
Will I not homeward go?
I fear traps high and low.

When I left home for here,
Sun and moon ushered in new year.
Now when may I go home?
Another year will come.
I sigh for I am lonely.
Why am I busy only?

Oh! how can I feel pleasure?
I toil without leisure.
Thinking of those in power,
Can I have any happy hour?
Don't I long for parental roof?
I'm afraid of reproof.

When I left for the west,
With warmth the sun and moon were blest.
When can I go home without cares,
Busy on state affairs?
It is late in the year;
They reap beans there and here.
I feel sad and cast down;
I eat the fruit I've sown.
Thinking of those in power,
I rise at early hours.
Will I not homeward go?
I fear returning blows.

Ah! officials in power,
There's no e'er-blooming flower.
When you're on duty long,
You can tell right from wrong.
If Heaven should have ear,
Justice would then appear.

Ah! officials in power,
There's no e'er resting hour.
If you do duty well,
You'd know heaven from hell.
If Heaven should hear you,
Blessings would come to view.

Note: An officer, kept long abroad on distant service, deplores the hardships
of his lot and complains about officials in power.

208. Music

The bells ring deep and low;
The vast river waves flow.
My heart is full of woe.
How can I forget then
Those music-making men!

The bells sound shrill and high;
The river waves flow by.
My heart heaves long, long sighs.
How can I forget then
Those music-loving men!

The bells and drums resound;
Three isles emerge, once drowned.
My heart feels grief profound.
How can I forget then
Those music-playing men!

They beat drums and ring bells,
Play lute and zither well,
In flute and pipe excel,
Sing odes and southern song
And dance with nothing wrong.

Note: This ode sings of those who play music so well that even the
once-drowned isles would emerge again at the sound of the music.

209. Winter Sacrifice

O let us clear away
    All the overgrown thorns!
Just as in olden day

We planted millet and corn.
Our millet overgrows
  And our barns stand in rows;
Our sorghum overgrows
  And our stacks stand in rows.
We prepare wine and meat
  For temple sacrifice;
We urge spirits to eat
  And invoke blessings thrice.

We clean the oxen nice
  And offer them in a heap
For winter sacrifice.
  We flay and broil the sheep
And cut and carve the meat.
  The priest's at temple gate
Till service is complete.
  Then come our fathers great.
They enjoy food and wine
  And to their grandsons say,
"Receive blessings divine,
  Live long and be e'er gay!"

The cooks work with great skill
  And prepare all the trays.
They roast or broil at will;
  Women help them always.
Smaller dishes abound
  For the guests left and right.
They raise cups and drink rounds
  According to the rite.
They laugh and talk at will
  When soothsayers come and say,
"Receive more blessings still;
  Live long with glee for aye!"

With respect we fulfil
　　The due rites one by one.
The priests announce the will
　　Of spirits to grandson:
"Fragrant's the sacrifice,
　　They enjoy meat and wine.
They confer blessings thrice
　　On you for rites divine.
You have done what is due
　　Correctly with good care.
Favors conferred on you
　　Will be found everywhere."

The ceremonies done,
　　Drums beaten and bells rung,
In his place the grandson,
　　The priest then gives his tongue:
"The spirits drunken well,
　　The dead ready to go."
Let's beat drums and ring bells
　　For them to go below!
Cooks and women come here!
　　Remove trays without delay!
Uncles and cousins dear,
　　At private feast let's stay!

Music played in the hall,
　　We eat when spirits go.
Enjoying dishes, all
　　Forget their former woe.
They drink their fill and eat,
　　Bowing the head, old and young.
"The spirits love your meat
　　And will make you live long.

Your rites are duly done;
    You are pious and nice.
Let no son nor grandson
    Forget the sacrifice!''

Note: This may be considered a hymn in the ''Book of Odes''. The ''spirit'' was a representative or impersonator of the worthy dead who was sacrificed to; the ''grandson'' was the name given to the sacrificer.

210. Spring Sacrifice

The Southern Mountain stands
Exploited by Yu's hands.
The plains spread high and low
Tilled by grandsons, crops grow.
Of southeast fields we find
The boundaries defined.

Clouds cover winter sky;
Snowflakes fall from on high.
In spring comes drizzling rain;
It moists and wets the plain.
Fertile grow all the fields;
Abundant are their yields.

Their acres lie in row;
Millet and sorghum grow.
Grandsons reap harvest fine
And make spirits and wine.
They feast their guests with food
That they may live for good.

Gourds grow amid the field
And melons have gross yield.

They are, pickled in slices,
Offered in sacrifices
That we may receive love
And long life from Heaven above.

We offer purest wine
To ancestors divine;
Kill a bull with red hair
With a knife in hand bare;
We rid it of hair red
And take fat from the bled.

During the sacrifice
The fat burned gives smell nice.
Our ancestors delight
In the service and rite.
We grandsons will be blest
With longest life and best.

Notice: It is supposed that this ode and the last proceeded from the same writer, this one being more concise on the subject of sacrifice and fuller on that of husbandry, which was traced to its first author, King Yu of Xia dynasty (2205–2197 BC).

(21) SIXTH DECADE OF ODES

211. Harvest

"Endless extend my boundless fields;
A tenth is levied on their yields.
I take grain from old stores
 To feed the peasants' mouth.
We've good years as of yore;
 I go to acres south.
They gather roots and weed;
 Lush grow millets I see.
Collected by those who lead,
 They are presented to me.

"I offer millets nice
And rams in sacrifice
To spirits of the land
 That lush my fields become.
Joyful my peasants stand;
 They play lutes and beat drums.
We pray to the God of Fields
 That rain and sunshine thrives
To increase our millet yields
 And bless my men and their wives."

Our lord's grandson comes near.
Our wives and children dear
Bring food to acres south.
The o'erseer opens his mouth
From left and right takes food
And tastes whether it's good.
Abundant millets grow
Over acres high and low.

Our lord's grandson is glad;
His peasants are not bad.

The grandson's crops in piles
Stand high as the roof tiles.
His stacks upon the ground
Look like hillock and mound.
He seeks stores in all parts
And conveys crops in carts.
We peasants sing in praise
Of millet, paddy, maize.
He'll be blessed night and day
And live happy for aye.

Note: This ode describes husbandry and sacrifices connected with it, and
happy understanding between the peasants and their lord, who is the speaker in the first two stanzas and the grandson (some think the overseer also)
in the third.

212. Farm Work

Busy with peasants' cares,
   Seed selected, tools repaired,
We take our sharp plough-shares
   When all is well prepared.
We begin from the south field
   And sow grain far and wide.
Gross and high grows our yield;
   Our lord's son is satisfied.

The grain's soft in the ear
   And then grows hard and good.
No grass nor weed appear;
   No insects eat it as food.
All vermins must expire

Lest they should do much harm.
The God puts them in fire
    To preserve our good farm.

Clouds gather in the sky;
    On public fields comes down.
Rain drizzles from on high,
    On private fields of our own.
There are unreaped young grain
    And some ungathered sheaves,
Handfuls left on the plain
    And ears a widow perceives
And gleans and makes a gain.

When our lord's son comes here,
    Our wives bring food to acres south
Together with their children dear.
    The o'erseer opens his mouth.
We offer sacrifice
    With victims black and red,
With millet and with rice.
    We pray to fathers dead
That we may   be blessed thrice.

Note: We have here further pictures of husbandry and sacrifices connected
with it. This ode is still fuller on the subject of husbandry than the last.

213. Grand Review

See River Luo in spring
    With water deep and wide.
Thither has come the king,
    Happy and dignified,
In red knee — covers new,
Six armies in review.

See River Luo in spring:
  Deep and wide flows its stream.
Thither has come the king;
  Gems on his scabbard gleam.
May he live long and gay,
His house preserved for aye!

See River Luo in spring;
  Its stream flows deep and wide.
Thither has come the king;
  He's blessed and dignified.
May he live long and great
And long preserve his state!

Note: This ode reads like a hymn sung by the feudal princes who meet at some gathering in the eastern capital by the side of River Luo and praise the king as he appears among them.

214. The Princes

Flowers give splendid sight
  With lush leaves by the side.
I see princes so bright;
  My heart is satisfied.
  My heart is satisfied;
I praise them with delight.

Flowers give splendid sight:
  They're deep yellow and red.
I see the princes so bright,
  Elegant and well-bred.
  Elegant and well-bred,
I bless them with delight.

Flowers give splendid sight:
   They're deep yellow and red.
I see the princes so bright,
   Elegant and well-bred.
   Elegant and well-bred,
I bless them with delight.

Flowers give splendid sight;
   They are yellow and white.
I see the princes so bright
   With four steeds left and right.
   With four steeds left and right,
They hold six reins with delight.

They go left if they will,
Driving the steeds with skill.
If they will they go right,
Driving with main and might.
Driving with skill their steeds,
They're one in words and deeds.

Note: This ode is said to respond to the previous one: the king celebrates the praises of the princes.

215. The Royal Toast

Hear the green-beaks' sweet voice
   And see their variegated wings fly!
Let all my lords rejoice
   And be blessed from on high!

Hear the green-beaks' sweet voice
   And see their feathers delicate!
Let all my lords rejoice
   And be buttress to the State!

Be a buttress or screen,
  Set an example fine,
Be self-restrained and keen,
  Receive blessings divine!

The cup of rhino horn
  Is filled with spirits soft.
Do not feel pride or scorn,
  And blessings will come oft.

Note: The king, entertaining his feudal princes, expresses his admiration and good wishes for them. The birds' sweet voice and feathers are intended to compliment the princes on the elegance of their manners.

216. To the Happily-Wed

Flying love-birds need rest
  With large and small nets spread.
May you live long and blessed,
  Wealthy and happily wed!

On the dam love-birds stay,
  In left wing hid the head.
May you live safe for aye,
  Duly and happily wed!

Four horses in the stable
  With grain and forage fed.
May you live long and stable,
  For you're happily wed!

Four horses in the stable
  With forage and grain fed.

May you live long and stable,
　　For you're happily wed!

Note: The writer wishes the newly-wed as faithful to each other as the love-birds. If either of a pair dies, the other is said to pine away and follow its mate to the grave from sorrow. The male and female do show an extraordinary attachment to each other, which is an emblem of conjugal fidelity. When love-birds sit or roost together, their heads are turned in opposite directions, bringing their left wings folded up so as to lean on each other, while their right wings are left at liberty to guard against any danger that may approach. A pair of love-birds seated on a dam in this position would be an instance of their mutual attachment. The four horses were used to draw the bride's carriage.

217. Family Banquet

Who are those lords so fine
　　In leather cap or hood?
Delicious is your wine
　　And your viands are good.
Can they be others?
They are your brothers.
They are like mistletoe
That o'er cypress does grow.
When they see you not, how
　　Can their hearts not be sad?
When they do see you now,
　　They are happy and glad.

Who are those lords so fine
　　In deer skin cap or hood?
Delicious is your wine;
　　Seasonable your food.
Can they be others?
They are your brothers.

They are like mistletoe
That o'er the pine does grow.
When they see you not, how
  Can their hearts not feel sad?
When they do see you now,
  They feel all right and glad.

Who are those lords so fine
  With leather cap on head?
Delicious is your wine,
  With food the table spread.
Oh! how can they be others?
They're our cousins and brothers.
We are like snow or rain;
Nothing will long remain.
Death may come any day.
How long can we together stay?
Drink and rejoice tonight at least!
Let us enjoy the feast!

Note: This ode is supposed to celebrate the king ("you") feasting with his relatives.

218. The Newly-Wed

Having prepared my creaking cart,
  I go to fetch my bride.
Not hungry nor thirsty at heart,
  I'll take her as good guide.
No good friend comes nor priest;
We'll rejoice in our feast.

In the plain there's dense wood
  And pheasants with long tails.

I love my young bride good;
  She'll help me without fail.
I'll praise her when we feast,
Never tired in the least.

Though we have no good wine,
  We'll drink and avoid waste.
Though our viand's not fine,
  We may give it a taste.
Though no good to you can I bring,
Still we may dance and sing.

I climb the mountain green
  To split oak for firewood.
Amid leaves lush and green
  I split oak for firewood.
Seeing my matchless bride,
I will be satisfied.

You're good like mountain high;
  Like the road you go long.
My four steeds run and hie;
  Six reins sing a lute-song.
I see my newly-wed;
With joy my heart's o'erspread.

Note: The bridegroom rejoices over his young, beautiful and virtuous bride.
Stanza 4 seems to mean that it is no easy thing to climb the mountain and
split the oak, but when accomplished, such a luxuriant tree repays the
labor. So it has not been an easy thing to get the bride, but now that she is
got, he forgets all the anxieties of his quest.

219. Slander

Hear the buzzing blue flies;
  On the fence they alight.
Lord, don't believe their lies;
  Friend, don't take wrong for right!

Hear blue flies buzzing, friend;
  They light on jujube trees.
The slander without end
  Spreads in the State disease.

Hear blue flies buzzing, friend;
  They light on hazel trees.
The slander without end
  Sets you at odds with me.

Note: This ode looks like a song against listening to slanders. The blue fly
has become symbolic of s slanderer.

220. Revelry

The guests come with delight,
And take places, left and right.
In rows arranged the dishes,
Displayed viands and fishes.
The wine is mild and good;
They drink and eat the food.
Bells and drums in their place,
They raise their cups with grace.
The target set on foot,
With bows for them to shoot,
The archers stand in row,
Ready their skill to show.

If the target is hit,
You'll drink a cup for it.

They dance to music sweet
Of flute and to drumbeat.
Rites are performed to please
Our ancestors with ease.
The offerings on hand
Are so full and so grand.
You will be richly blessed,
Sons, grandsons and the rest.
Happy is every man.
Let each do what he can!
Each guest shoots with his bow;
The host joins in the row.
Let us fill every cup!
When one hits, all cheer up.

When guests begin to feast,
They are gentle at least.
When they've not drunk too much,
    They would observe the rite;
When they have drunk too much,
    Their deportment is light.
They leave their seats and go
Capering to and fro.
When they've not drunk too much,
    They are in a good mood;
When they have drunk too much,
    They're indecent and rude.
When they are deeply drunk,
They know not where they've sunk.

When they've drunk their cups dry,
They shout out, brawl and cry.

They put plates upside down;
They dance like funny clowns.
When they have drunk wine strong,
They know not right from wrong.
With their caps on one side,
They dance and slip and slide.
If drunk they went away,
The host would happy stay.
But drunk they will not go;
The host is full of woe.
We may drink with delight
If we observe the rite.

Whenever people drink,
In drunkenness some sink.
Appoint an inspector
And keep a register!
But drunkards feel no shame;
On others they'll lay blame.
Do not drink more toasts,
Or they will wrong the host!
Do not speak if you could;
Say only what you should!
Don't say like drunkard born
You're a ram without horn!
With three cups you've lost head;
With more you'd be drunk dead.

Note: This is an ode against drunkenness, in which we find a lively picture
of the licence of the times. In Stanzas 1 and 2 we have two instances of the
temperate use of spirits at trials of archery before the king, and in 3—5 we
have the abuse of them on festive occasions.

(22) SEVENTH DECADE OF ODES

221. The King

The fish among the weeds,
Showing large head, swims with speed.
The king in the capital
Drinks happy in the hall.

The fish swims thereamong,
Showing its tail so long.
The king in the capital
Drinks cheerfully in the hall.

The fish among the weed
Sheltered by rush and reed,
The king in the capital
Dwells carefree in the hall.

Note: This is a praise of the king by the princes at some feast. The fish is in its proper place, enjoying what happiness it could enjoy, and so it serves to indicate how the king enjoys himself in his capital.

222. Royal Favors

Gather beans long and short
    In baskets round and square.
The lords come to the court.
    What suitable things there
Can be given to meet their needs?
    A state cab and horses four.
What else besides the steeds?

Dragon robes they adore.

Gather cress long and short
  Around the spring near by.
The lords come to the court;
  I see dragon flags fly.
Flags flutter in the breeze,
  Three or four horses run
And bells ring without cease,
  The lords come one by one.

Red covers on their knees
  And their buskins below.
They go with perfect ease
  In what the king bestows.
They receive with delight
  High favors from the king;
They receive with delight
  Good fortune in a string.

On branches of oak-tree,
  What riot lush leaves run!
The lords guard with high glee
  The land of Heaven's Son.
They receive with delight
  Blessings from high and low.
Attendants left and right
  Follow them where they go.

The boat of willow wood
  Fastened by band or rope,
Of happy lords and good
  The king scans the full scope.
They receive with high glee
  All blessings from the king.

They're happy and carefree;
  Fortune comes on the wing.

Note: This ode responds to the previous one, celebrating the appearance of
the feudal princes at the court, the splendor of their array, the propriety of
their demeanour and the favors conferred on them by the king.

223. Admonition

Tighten the string of the bow,
  Its recoil will be swift.
If brothers alien go,
  Their affection will shift.

If you alienate
  Your relatives and brothers,
People will imitate
  You when they deal with others.

When there is brotherhood,
  Good feeling is displayed.
When brothers are not good,
  Much trouble will be made.

When people have no grace,
  They blame the other side;
They fight to get high place
  And come to fratricide.

Old steeds think themselves good;
  Of the young they don't think.
They want plenty of food
  And an excess of drink.

Don't teach apes to climb trees
    Nor add mud to the wall!
If you do good with ease,
    They'll follow you one and all.

Flake on flake falls the snow;
    It dissolves in the sun.
Don't despise those below!
    The proud will be undone.

The snow falls flake on flake;
    It will melt in sunlight.
Let no barbarians make
    You fall into a sad plight!

Note: This was directed against the king's cold treatment of his relatives and his encouragement of slanderers. When the bow is drawn, all its parts are brought near to the archer; when he lets the arrow go, it returns to its former state and is far off from him. So it is between the Head of a House and his relatives. He should draw them to himself. If he relax the hold of his kindness upon them, they recoil from him.

224. An Unjust Lord

Lush is the willow tree.
    Who won't rest under it?
Our lord's to punish free.
    Don't fall into the pit!
You lend him hand and arm,
But he will do you harm.

Lush is the willow tree.
    Who won't shelter 'neath it?
Our lord's to punish free;
    His ire bursts in a fit.

You lend him arm and hand;
He'll ban you from the land.

The bird flies as it can
    Even up to the sky.
The heart of such a man
    Will go up far and high.
Whate'er for him you do,
He's free to punish you.

Note: The writer tells how impossible it was to approach or do anything for the unjust King Li (877—841 BC). A willow tree is an object inviting the traveller to rest under its shadow, so should the king have been, affording shelter to all the people. But it was not so.

225. Men of Old Capital

Men of old capital
    In yellow fox-fur dress,
With face unmoved at all,
    Spoke with pleasing address.
At the old capital
They were admired by all.

Men of old capital
    Wore their hat up-to-date,
And noble ladies tall
    Had hair so thick and straight.
Although I see them not,
Could their face be forgot?

Men of old capital
    Wore pendant from the ear,
And noble ladies tall
    Were fair without a peer.

Although I see them not,
Could their dress be forgot?

Men of old capital
   With girdle hanging down
And noble ladies tall
   With hair like tail of scorpion.
Of them could I see one,
After them I would run.

His girdle hanging there
   Suited so well his gown;
Her natural curled hair
   Was wavy up and down.
I see not their return.
How much for them I yearn!

Note: This is an ode in praise of the lords and ladies of the old capital,
written after King Ping removed the capital to the east in 770 BC.

226. My Lord Not Back

I gather all the morn king-grass,
But get not a handful, alas!
In a wisp is my hair,
I'll go home and wash it with care.

I gather all the morn plants indigo,
But get not an apronful, Oh!
Within five days my lord is due;
Now it's the sixth, I feel so blue.

If he should hunting go,
I would put in its case his bow.

If he should go to fish,
I'd arrange his line at his wish.

What would we take out of the stream?
O tench and bream.
O tench and bream,
With what wild joy my face would beam!

Note: This ode reads rather like a song which should have been collected in the "Book of Lyrics". A wife tells her sorrow and her inability to attend to anything in the prolonged absence of her husband to whom she was fondly attached.

227. Journey Home

Young millet grows tall and strong,
Fattened by genial rain.
Our southward journey's long;
The Lord of Zhao cheers the train.

Our carts go one by one;
Our oxen follow the track.
Our construction is done.
So we are going back.

We go on foot or run;
Our host goes in a throng.
Our construction is done,
So we are going along.

The town of Xie stands strong,
Built by our lord with might and main.
Our expedition's long
And our lord leads the train.

Lowland becomes a plain;
    Streams are cleared east and west.
Our lord leads the campaign;
    The king's heart is at rest.

Note: This ode celebrates the service of the Duke of Zhao in building the city of Xie for the marquisate of Shen established by King Xuan (826−781 BC) as a bulwark against the encroachments of wild tribes.

228. My Love

In lowland mulberry tree's fair;
    Its leaves are lush and bright.
When I see my love there,
    How great will be my delight!

In lowland mulberry tree's fair;
    Its leaves shed glossy light.
When I seemy love there,
    How can I not feel delight?

In lowland mulberry tree's fair;
    Its leaves are dark each day.
When I see my love there,
    How much have I to say?

I love him in my heart,
    Why won't I tell him so?
Better keep it apart
    That sweeter it will grow.

Note: It is thought that this ode should have been arranged in the "Book of Lyrics". A woman speaks of her admiration and love for a man fair as the mulberry tree and bright as its leaves.

229. The Degraded Queen

White flowered rushes sway
   Together with white grass.
My lord sends me away
   And leaves me alone, alas!

White clouds with dew-drops spray
   Rushes and grass all o'er.
Hard is the skyward way;
   My lord loves me no more.

Northward the stream goes by,
   Flooding the ricefields there.
With wounded heart I sigh,
   Thinking of his mistress fair.

We cut wood from the tree
   To make fire in the stove.
His mistress fair makes me
   Lose the heart of my love.

When rings the palace bell,
   Its sound is heard without.
When I think of him well,
   I hear but angry shout.

The heron may eat fish
   While the crane hungry goes.
His mistress has her wish
   While I am full of woes.

The lovebirds on the dam
   Hide their beak 'neath left wing.
The woe in which I am,

Is what my lord did bring.

Thin is that slab of stone;
　　Who stands on it stands low.
My lord leaves me alone;
　　My heart is full of woe.

Note: The Queen of King You (reigned 780−770 BC) complains of being degraded and forsaken as her husband preferred his concubine, Lady Bao Shi. The first two lines suggest the idea of the close connection between the two plants and the necessity of the one to the other, as it should be between husband and wife. But the king sends the queen away and leaves her alone. The idea in stanza 2 seems to be that the clouds bestow their dewy influences on the smallest plants, while the king neglects the queen. The idea in stanza 3 is that the flooding of the rice-fields is the greatest benefit to them; not so does the king deal with his queen. Both the birds in stanza 6 live on fish, but the crane is a clean bird and the heron an unclean one. Here, however, the crane is in the forest where it would be famished, and the heron is on the dam where it could have its fill. So have the queen and the concubine changed places. It is supposed that by the "thin slab stone" in the last stanza Lady Bao Shi is intended. The king is meant by the person standing on the thin stone, favoring the concubine and yet only made to appear mean and low by his connection with her.

230. Hard Journey

O hear the oriole's song!
　　It rests on mountain slope.
The journey's hard and long.
　　How can a tired man cope?
Give me food and be kind,
　　Help me, encourage me,
Tell the carriage behind
　　To stop and carry me!

O hear the oriole's song!

It rests at mountain yon.
Do I fear journey long?
  I fear I can't go on.
Give me food and be kind,
  Help me, encourage me,
Tell the carriage behind
  To stop and carry me!

O hear the oriole's song!
  It rests at mountain's bend.
Do I fear journey long?
  I can't get to its end.
Give me food and be kind,
  Help me, encourage me,
Tell the carriage behind
  To stop and carry me!

Note: A toiler complains of the hard journey. The oriole has its proper place in which to rest, but not so is it with the speaker, who is left neglected, though exhausted with toil.

231. Frugal Hospitality

The waving gourd leaves are fine,
  Taken and boiled in haste.
Our good friend has sweet wine;
  He pours it out for a taste.

The rabbit's meat is fine
  When baked or roasted up.
Our good friend has sweet wine;
  He presents us a cup.

The rabbit's meat is fine

When broiled or roasted up.
Our good friend has sweet wine;
We present him a cup.

The rabbit's meat is fine
When baked or roasted up.
Our good friend has sweet wine;
We fill each other's cup.

Note: This ode describes the simple manners and decency of an earlier time, showing that where the provisions are most frugal, all the rules of polite intercourse may yet be preserved. For no supply of vegetables at a meal could be more frugal than boiled gourd leaves, and no supply of viands more frugal than a single rabbit. Line 2 in stanzas 2 – 4 gives the different ways in which the rabbit might be cooked: baked in the ashes, roasted near the fire or broiled over the fire.

232. Eastern Expedition

The mountain frowns
With rocky crowns.
Peaks high, streams long,
Toilsome the throng.
Warriors east go;
No rest they know.

The mountain frowns
With craggy crowns.
Peaks high, streams bend.
When is the end?
Warriors go east.
When to be released?

White-footed swines wade
Through streams and fade.

In Hyades the moon
Foretells hard rain soon.
Warriors east go;
No plaint they show.

Note: This ode recalls the hardships of a long and difficult expedition to the east, aggravated by heavy rains. It may be ascribed to the reign of King Li (877 — 841 BC). It is the nature of the swine to wallow in the mire, and even those of them who may have white feet become so dirty that it cannot be seen that they have white feet; but now the soldiers saw the white feet of the swine and that they were in crowds wading in the waters — much rain had fallen and the pools lay deep all over the country. The moon's rising in Hyades is supposed to be an indication that there will soon be great rain. Therefore, the warriors' thoughts were all occupied with the calamity of the rain which had fallen and was likely to fall still more heavily so that they had not time to think of anything else.

233. Famine

The bignonia blooms
Yellow and fade.
My heart is full of gloom;
I feel the wound grief's made.

The bignonia blooms
Have left the green leaves dry.
Could I foretell what looms,
I would not live but die.

The ewe's lean; large its head.
In fish-trap there's no fish.
Some people may be fed;
Few can get what they wish.

Note: The writer laments the famine and misery in consequence of a general decay of the kingdom. When the bignonia's flowers are about to fall, they turn to a deep yellow, and in this the writer sees an emblem of the decaying condition of the House of Zhou. He could do nothing but grieve over the state of things. In the last stanza the ewe is so emaciated that its head appears extraordinarily large, and there is no fish in the trap so that the stars appear clearly reflected in it. The waters do not yield the usual supplies of food to men.

234. Poor Soldiers

Nowhere but yellow grass,
   Not a day have we rest.
No soldier but should pass
   Here and there, east or west.

Nowhere but rotten grass,
   None but has left his wife.
We poor soldiers, alas!
   Lead an inhuman life.

We're not tigers nor beast.
   Why in the wilds do we stay?
Alas! we're men at least.
   Why toil we night and day?

Unlike the long-tailed foxes
   Deep hidden in the grass,
In our carts with our boxes
   We toil our way, alas!

Note: This ode describes the misery of the soldiers in the time of King You (780 – 770 BC), who were constantly employed in expeditionary service and treated like rotten yellow grass. It is natural for tigers to be found in the wilds and for foxes to be hidden among the long, dark grass, but not for these poor soldiers to be employed as they were.

Part III

Book of Epics

Part III

Book of Epics

(23) FIRST DECADE OF EPICS

235. Heaven's Decree

King Wen rests in the sky;
His spirit shines on high.
Though Zhou is an old State,
It's destined to be great.
The House of Zhou is bright;
God brings it to the height.
King Wen will e'er abide
At God's left or right side.

King Wen was good and strong;
His fame lasts wide and long.
God's gifts to Zhou will run
From his son to grandson.
Descendants of his line
Will receive gifts divine;
So will talents and sage
Be blest from age to age.

From age to age they're blest;
They work with care and zest.
Brilliant, they dedicate
Their lives to the royal State.
Born in this royal land,
They'll support the house grand.
With talents standing by,
King Wen may rest on high.

King Wen was dignified,
Respected far and wide.
At Heaven's holy call

The sons of Shang come all.
Those sons of the noblesse
Of Shang are numberless.
As Heaven orders it,
They cannot but submit.

Submission's nothing strange;
Heaven's decree may change.
They were Shang's officers;
They're now Zhou's servitors.
They serve wine in distress,
In Shang cap and Yin dress.
You loyal ministers,
Don't miss your ancestors!

Miss no ancestors dear;
Cultivate virtue here!
Obey Heaven's decree
And you'll live in high glee.
Ere it lost people's heart,
Yin played its ordained part.
From Yin's example we see
It's hard to keep decree.

O keep Heaven's decree
Or you will cease to be!
Let virtue radiate;
Profit from Yin's sad fate!
All grow under the sky
Silently far and nigh.
Take pattern from King Wen!
All States will obey you then.

Note: This is the first epic ode celebrating King Wen (1184−1134 BC) as
the founder of the Zhou dynasty. It was attributed to the Duke of Zhou for
the benefit of the young King Cheng (1114−1076 BC). It shows how King

Wen's virtues drew to him the favor of Heaven and made him a bright pattern for his descendants and their ministers. Stanza 5 carries on the subject of the descendants of the previous dynasty called first Shang and then Yin. When they appeared at the court of Zhou, they assisted at the sacrifices of the king in his ancestral temple, which began with a libation of fragrant spirits to bring down the Spirits of the departed. The libation was poured out by the representative of the dead and the cup with the spirits was handed to him by Yin officers.

236. Three Kings of Zhou

Gods know on high
 What's done below.
We can't rely
 On grace they show.
It's hard to retain
 The royal crown.
Yin-Shang did reign;
 It's overthrown.

Ren, Princess Yin,
 Left Shang's town-wall
To marry in
 Zhou's capital.
She wed King Ji,
 The best of men.
Then pregnant, she
 Gave birth to Wen.

When he was crowned,
 Wen served with care
The gods around,
 Blessed here and there.
His virtue's great,
 Fit head of the State.

Heaven above
  Ruled o'er our fate.
It chose with love
  For Wen a mate.
On sunny side
  Of River Wei
Wen found his bride
  In rich array.

Born in a large State,
  The celestial bride
And auspicious mate,
  Stood by the riverside.
On a bridge of boats they met,
Splendor ne'er to forget.

At Heaven's call
  Wen again wed
In capital
  Xin nobly-bred.
She bore a son
  Who should take down,
When victory's won,
  The royal crown.

Shang's troops did wield
Forest-like flags afield.
Wu took oath on the Plain
To start the campaign:
"God's overhead.
Don't shrink in dread!"

The battlefield's wide,
  War chariots strong,
The steeds we ride

Gallop along.
Our Master Jiang
  Assists the king
To overthrow the Shang
  Like an eagle on the wing.
A morning bright
Displaced the night.

Note : This epic ode celebrates King Ji who married Princess Ren of Yin,
King Wen who married Xin, and King Wu who overthrew the dynasty of
Shang in 1121 BC.

237. The Migration in 1325 BC

Gourds grow in long, long trains;
Our people grew in the plains.
They moved to Qi from Tu,
Led by old Duke Tan Fu,
And built kilnlike hut and cave
But house they did not have.

Tan Fu took morning ride;
Along the western side
Of River Wei came he
To the foot of Mount Qi;
His wife Jiang came at his right
To find a housing site.

Zhou plain spread at his feet
With plants and violets sweet.
He asked his men their mind,
And by tortoise shell divined.
He was told there to stay
And build homes right away.

They settled at the site
And planned to build left and right.
They divided the ground
And dug ditches around
From west to east there was no land
But Tan Fu took in hand.

He named two officers
In charge of laborers
To build their houses fine.
They made walls straight with the line
And bound the frame-boards tight.
A temple rose in sight.

They brought basketfuls of earth
And cast it in frames with mirth.
Then they beat it with blows
And pared the walls in rows.
A hundred walls did rise;
Drums were drowned in their cries.

They set up city gate;
It stood so high and straight.
They set up palace door
They'd never seen before.
They reared an altar grand
To spirits of the land.

The angry foe not tame
Feared our Duke Tan Fu's name.
Oaks and thorns cleared away,
People might go their way.
The savage hordes in flight
Panted and ran out of sight.

The lords no longer strove;
King Wen taught them to love.
E'en strangers became kind;
They followed him behind.
He let all people speak
And defended the weak.

Note: This epic ode narrates the beginning and subsequent growth of the
House of Zhou, its removal from Bin under Duke Tan Fu in 1325 BC and
its settlement in the plain of Zhou, down to the time of King Wen. We have
here an eloquent account of Tan Fu's labors in founding the new settlement. Duke Liu, to whom is ascribed the previous settlement of the tribe
in Bin in 1796 BC, is celebrated in epics or ode 250.

238. King Wen of Zhou

Oak trees and shrubs lush grow;
They'll make firewood in a row.
Our king has talents bright
To serve him left and right.

Our king has talents bright
To hold cups left and right.
They offer sacrifice
And pour libations nice.

On River Jin afloat
Many a ship and boat,
The king orders to fight
Six hosts of warriors bright.

The Milky Way on high
Makes figure in the sky.
Our king lives a life long

And breeds talents in throng.

Figures by chisels made
Look like metal or jade.
Our king so active stands;
He rules over the lands.

Note: This ode celebrates King Wen's activity, influence and capacity to
rule by using talents, who are compared to oak trees in the first stanza. Stanza 2 describes the grave formality with which the officers standing on the
chief's left and right go through their business. Stanza 3 shows that only the
king leads six armies (hosts) into the field. In stanza 4 the king arranges the
orders of nobility, making the earth glorious as the Milky Way does the
sky. Stanza 5 seems to be allusive of the state of the kingdom made goodly
and great by the king like the most precious substances, gold and jade,
wrought on by skilful workmen.

239. Our Prince

At the mountain's foot, lo!
How lush the hazels grow!
Our prince is self-possessed
And he prays to be blessed.

The cup of jade is fine,
O'erflowing with yellow wine.
Our prince is self-possessed;
He prays and he is blessed.

The hawks fly in the sky;
The fish leap in the deep.
Our prince is self-possessed;
He prays his men be blessed.

Jade cups of wine are full;

Ready is the red bull.
He pays the sacred rite
To increase blessings bright.

Oaks grow in the neighborhood;
They are used for firewood.
Our prince is self-possessed;
By gods he's cheered and blessed.

How the creeper and vine
Around the branches twine!
Our prince is self possessed;
He prays right and he's blessed.

Note: The prince prays at the mountain's foot favorable to vegetable growth, using a jade cup proper for yellow wine. He prays that his men be blessed like hawks flying in the sky and fish leaping in the deep. A red bull is used as victim for sacrifice, for red is the color of honor in the Zhou dynasty. As it is natural for oaks to grow and for creepers and vines to twine around their branches, so is it for the prince and his talented men to be blessed.

240. King Wen's Reign

Reverent Lady Ren
Was mother of King Wen.
She loved grandmother dear,
A good wife without peer.
Si inherited her fame;
From her a hundred sons came.

Good done to fathers dead,
Nowhere complaint was spread,
They reposed as they could.
King Wen set example good

To his dear wife and brothers,
His countrymen and others.

At home benevolent,
In temple reverent,
He had gods e'er in view
And did what he should do.

All evils rectified,
No ill done far and wide.
Untaught, he knew the right;
Unadvised, he saw the light.

The grown-up became good;
E'en the young showed manhood.
All talents sang in praise
Of King Wen's olden days.

Note: This is an epic ode in praise of the virtue of King Wen and the excellent character of his mother Ren and his wife Si.

241. The Rise of the Zhou

O God is great!
He saw our State,
Surveyed our land
And saw how people stand.
Dissatisfied
With Yin-Shang's side,
Then he would fain
Find out again
Another state
He did not hate.
His eyes turned west;

Our State was blest.

Tai cut the head
Off the trunk dead
And hewed with blows
The bushy rows.
The rotten trees
And mulberries
Were cleared away
Or put in array.
God made the road
For men's abode.
King Tai was made
Heaven's sure aide.

God visited Mount Qi
And thinned oak tree on tree.
Cypress and pines stood straight;
God founded the Zhou State.
He chose Tai as its head
And Ji when Tai was dead.
Ji loved his brothers dear;
His heart was full of cheer.
When Ji was head of State,
He made its glory great.
The House of Zhou was blest
North to south, east to west.

God gave King Ji
The power to see
Clearly right from wrong
That he might rule for long.
With intelligence great
He could lead the whole State;
He ruled with wisdom high,

Thus obeyed far and nigh.
In his son King Wen's days
People still sang his praise.
For God's blessings would run
To his son and grandson.

To our King Wen God said,
"Don't let the foe invade
Your holy land with might!
First occupy the height!"
The Mi tribe disobeyed,
On our land made a raid,
Attacked Yuan and Gong State;
King Wen's anger was great.
He sent his troops in rows
To stop invading foes
That the Zhou House might stand
And rule over the land.

The capital gave order
To attack from Yuan border
And occupy the height.
Let no foe come with might
Near our hill or our mountain.
Nor to drink from our fountain
Nor our pools filled by rain!
King Wen surveyed the plain,
Settled and occupied
Hillside and riverside.
As great king he would stand
For people and the land.

To our King Wen God said,
"High virtue you've displayed.
You're ever lenient

To deal out punishment.
Making no effort on your part,
You follow me at heart."
To our King Wen God said,
"Consult allied brigade,
Attack with brethren strong,
Use scaling ladders long
And engines of assault
To punish Chong State's fault!"

The engines of onfall
Attacked the Chong State wall.
Many captives were ta'en
And left ears of the slain.
Sacrifice made afield,
We called the foe to yield.
  None dare insult Zhou State.
The engines of onfall
Destroyed the Chong State wall.
The foe filled with dismay,
Their forces swept away,
  None dare disobey our king great.

Note: This epic ode shows the rise of the House of Zhou as a sovereign kingdom and the achievements of King Tai, King Ji and especially King Wen
who conquered the Mi tribe and the Chong State in 1135 BC.

242. The Wondrous Park

When the tower began
To be built, every man
Took part as if heated,
The work was soon completed.
"No hurry," said the king,

But they worked as his offspring.

In Wondrous Park the king
Saw the deer in the ring
Lie at his left and right;
How sweet sang the birds white!
The king by Wondrous Pond
Saw fishes leap and bound.

In water-girded hall
Beams were long and posts tall.
Drums would beat and bells ring
To amuse our good king.

Drums would beat and bells ring
To amuse our good king.
The lizard-skin drums beat;
Blind musicians sang sweet.

Note: This ode shows the joy of the people in the growing opulence and dignity of King Wen, who moved his capital to Feng after the overthrow of the
State of Chong in 1135 BC, only one year before his death.

243. King Wu

In Zhou successors rise;
All of them are kings wise.
To the three kings in heaven
King Wu in Hao is given.

King Wu in Hao is given
To the order of Heaven.
He would seek virtue good
To attain true kinghood.

To attain true kinghood,
Be filial a man should.
He'd be pattern for all;
"Be filial" is his call.

All people love King Wu;
What they are told, they do.
Be filial a man should;
The bright successor's good.

All bright successors good
Follow their fatherhood.
For long they will be given
The blessings of good Heaven.

The blessings of good Heaven
And good Earth will be given
For long years without end
To the people's great friend.

Note: This is an ode in praise of King Wu (reigned 1121 – 1115 BC), who walked in the ways of his forefathers, and by his filial piety secured the throne for himself and his posterity.

244. Kings Wen and Wu

King Wen had great fame
And famous he became.
He sought peace in the land
And saw it peaceful stand.
Oh! King Wen was so grand.

King Wen whom gods did bless

Achieved martial success.
Having overthrown Chong,
He fixed his town at Fong.
Oh! may King Wen live long!

King Wen built moat and wall
Around the capital
Not for his own desire
But for those of his sire.
Oh! our prince we admire!

King Wen at capital
Strong as the city wall,
The lords from State to State
Paid homage to prince great.
Our royal prince was great.

The River Feng east flowed;
Our thanks to Yu we owed.
The lords from land to land
Paid homage to king grand.
How great King Wu did stand!

He built water-girt hall
At Hao the capital.
From north to south, from east to west,
By people he was blest.
King Wu was at his crest.

The king divined the site;
The tortoise-shell foretold it right
To build the palace hall
At Hao the capital.
King Wu was admired by all.

By River Feng white millet grew.
How could talents not serve King Wu?
All that he'd planned and done
Was for his son and grandson.
King Wu was second to none.

Note: This is an ode in praise of Kings Wen and Wu. The first four stanzas
show how King Wen displayed his military prowess to secure the tranquility
of the people and how this was manifested in the building of Feng (or Fong
in stanza 2) as his capital city. In stanza 5, Yu refers to the founder of the
Xia dynasty (reigned 2205 – 2197 BC). The last four stanzas show King Wu
in his capital of Hao.

(24) SECOND DECADE OF EPICS

245. Hou Ji, the Lord of Corn

Who gave birth to the Lord of Grain and Corn?
By Lady Jiang Yuan he was born.
How gave she birth to her son nice?
She went afield for sacrifice.
Unmarried, childless did she go;
She trod on the print of Divine toe.
She stood there long and took a rest,
And she was aggrandized and blessed.
Then she conceived, then she gave birth,
It was the Lord of Grain and Corn on earth.

When her carrying time was done,
Like a lamb was born her first son.
Of labor she suffered no pain;
She was not hurt, nor did she strain.
How could his birth so wonderful be?
Was it against Heaven's decree?
Was God displeased with her sacrifice
To give a virgin a son nice?

The son abandoned in a lane
  Was milked by the cow or sheep.
Abandoned in a wooded plain,
  He's fed by men in forest deep.
Abandoned on the coldest ice,
  He was warmed by birds with their wings.
When flew away those birds so nice,
  The cry was heard of the nursling's.
He cried and wailed so long and loud
The road with his voice was o'erflowed.

He was able to crawl aground
  And then rose to his feet.
When he sought food around,
  He learned to plant large beans and wheat.
The beans he planted grew tall;
  His millet grew in rows;
His gourds teemed large and small;
  His hemp grew thick and close.

The Lord of Corn knew well the way
  To help the growing of the grain.
He cleared the grasses rank away
  And sowed with yellow seed the plain.
The new buds began to appear;
  They sprang up, grew under the feet.
They flowered and came into ear;
  They drooped down, each grain complete.
They became so good and so strong,
Our Lord would live at Tai for long.

Heaven gave them the lucky grains
  Of double-kernelled millet black
And red and white ones on the plains.
  Black millet reaped was piled in stack
Or carried back on shoulders bare.
  Red and white millet growing nice
And reaped far and wide, here and there,
  Was brought home for the sacrifice.

What is our sacrifice?
We hull and ladle rice,
We sift and tread the grain,
Swill and scour it again.
It's steamed and then distilled;

We see the rites fulfilled.
We offer fat with southernwood
And a skinned ram as food.
Roast and broiled flesh with cheer
Brings good harvest next year.

We load the stands with food,
The stands of earthernware or wood.
God smells its fragrance rise;
He's well pleased in the skies.
What smell is this, so nice?
It's our Lord's sacrifice.
This is a winning way;
It's come down to this day.

Note: This is a legendary ode in praise of Hou Ji, the Lord of Grain or
Corn, founder of the House of Zhou.

246. Banquet

Let no cattle and sheep
    Trample on roadside rush
Which bursts up with root deep
    And with leaves soft and lush.
We're closely related brothers.
    Let us be seated near.
Spread mats for some; for others
    Stools will be given here.

Mats spread one on another,
    Servants come down and up.
Host and guests pledge each other;
    They rinse and fill their cup.
Sauce brought with prickles ripe

And roast or broiled meat,
There are provisions of tripe,
   All sing to music sweet.

The bow prepared is strong
And the four arrows long.
The guests all try to hit
And stand in order fit.
They fully draw the bow
And four arrows straight go.
They hit like planting trees;
Those who miss stand at ease.

The grandson is the host;
With sweet or strong wine they toast.
They drink the cups they hold
And pray for all the old.
The hoary old may lead
And help the young in need.
May their old age be blest;
May they enjoy their best!

Note: This ode celebrates an entertainment given by the king (grandson) to his relatives, with an archery competition after the feast; it also celebrates the honor done on such occasion to the aged.

247. Sacrificial Ode

We've drunk wine strong
   And thank your grace.
May you live long!
   Long live your race!

We've drunk wine strong

And eaten food.
May you live long!
Be wise and good!

Be good and wise
From end to end!
See Spirit rise
And speak for our dead friend.

What does he say?
Your food is fine.
Constant friends stay
At the service divine.

With constant friends
And filial sons
There won't be ends
For pious ones.

To you belong
The pious race.
May you live long;
Be blest with grace!

Your race appears
By Heaven blest.
You'll live long years,
Served east and west.

Who will serve you?
You will have maids and men.
Their sons will renew
Their service again.

Note: This ode is responsive to the last, the first three stanzas sung by the
king's relatives and the last five by the personator of the dead.

248. The Ancestor's Spirit

On the stream waterbirds appear;
  On earth descends the Spirit good.
Your wine is sweet and clear;
  And fragrant is your food.
The Spirit comes to drink and eat;
Your blessing will be sweet.

On the sand waterbirds appear;
  On earth enjoys the Spirit good.
Abundant is your wine clear;
  Delicious is your food.
The Spirit comes to drink and eat;
Your blessing will be complete.

On the isle waterbirds appear;
  In his place sits the Spirit good.
Your wine is pure and clear;
  In slices are your meat and food.
The Spirit eats and drinks sweet wine;
You will receive blessing divine.

Waterbirds swim where waters meet;
  The spirit sits in a high place.
In his high place he drinks wine sweet;
  You will receive blessing and grace.
The Spirit drinks and eats his food;
You'll receive blessing doubly good.

In the gorge waterbirds appear;
  Drunken on earth the Spirit good.
Delicious is your wine clear;
  Broiled and roast your meat and food.

The Spirit comes to drink and feast;
You'll have no trouble in the least.

Note: This is an ode appropriate for the feast given to the personator of the
departed on the day after the sacrifice in the ancestral temple. The
waterbirds enjoy themselves on the stream, sand, isle and in the gorge; the
personator may relax from the gravity of the preceding day and be happy.

249. King Cheng

Happy and good our king,
Of his virtue all sing.
He's good to people all;
On him all blessings fall
And favor from on high
Is renewed far and nigh.

They are blessed, everyone
Of his sons and grandsons.
He's majestic and great,
Fit ruler of the State.
Blameless and dutiful,
He follows fathers' rule.

His bearing dignified,
His virtue spreads far and wide.
From prejudice he's free,
Revered by all with glee.
He receives blessings great,
Modeled on from State to State.

He's modeled on without end;
Each State becomes his friend.
Ministers all and one
Admire the Heaven's Son.

Dutiful, he is blest;
In him people find rest.

Note: This is an ode in praise of King Cheng (1114 – 1076 BC), who succeeded King Wu at the age of thirteen with the Duke of Zhou as regent.

250. Duke Liu

Duke Liu was blest;
He took no ease nor rest.
He divided the fields
And stored in barns the yields.
In bags and sacks he tied
Up grain and meat when dried;
He led people in rows,
With arrows and drawn bows.
With axes, shields and spears,
They marched on new frontiers.

Duke Liu would fain
Survey a fertile plain
For his people to stay.
On that victorious day
None would sigh without rest.
He came up mountain-crest
And descended again.
We saw his girdle then
Adorned with gems and jade,
His precious sword displayed.

Duke Liu crossed the mountains
And saw a hundred fountains.
He surveyed the plain wide
By the southern hillside.

He found a new capital
Wide for his people all.
Some thought it good for the throng;
Others would not dwell there for long.
There was discussion free;
They talked in high glee.

Duke Liu was blest;
At capital he took rest,
Put stools on mats he spread
For officers he led.
They leant on stools and sat
On the ornamented mat.
A penned pig was killed;
Their gourds with wine were filled.
Theye were well drunk and fed
And hailed him as State head.

Duke Liu would fain
Measure the hill and plain
Broad and long; he surveyed
Streams and springs, light and shade;
His three armies were placed
By the hillside terraced;
He measured plains anew
And fixed the revenue.
Fields were tilled in the west;
The land of Bin was blest.

Duke Liu who wore the crown
At Bin had settled down.
He crossed the River Wei
To gather stones by day.
All boundaries defined,
People worked with one mind

On the Huang Riverside
Toward Guo River wide.
The people dense would stay
On the shore of the Ney.

Note: This epic ode tells the story of how Duke Liu, who had been living previously in Tai (the principality with which Hou Ji, the Lord of Corn, was invested by Emperor Yao of Tang in 2276 BC) was driven out of it in 1796 BC when the rule of Xia was in great disorder. Duke Liu made his first settlement in Bin at the foot of Mount Ji about 100 li west of Tai, building there, laying out the ground, forming armies and arranging for a revenue till Bin became too small for all his people. The composition of this ode is ascribed to Duke Kang of Zhao, who is said to have made it for King Cheng when he was about to undertake the duties of the government.

251. Duke Kang of Zhao's Admonition

Take water from pools far away,
Pour it in vessels that it may
Be used to steam millet and rice.
A prince should give fraternal advice
Like parent to his people nice.

Take water from pools far away,
Pour it in vessels that it may
Be used to wash the spirit-vase.
A prince should give fraternal praise
To his people for better days.

Take water from pools far away,
Pour it in vessels that it may
Be used to cleanse everything.
To our fraternal prince or king
Like water his people will cling.

Note: Pool-water purified may be used in sacrifice as for other purposes.
The most unlikely things may be made useful by human ingenuity; how
much more should a sovereign fulfill the duties of his position. This ode, like
the last, and also the one that follows, are attributed to the Duke of Zhao,
as made by him for the admonition of King Cheng.

252. King Cheng's Excursion

The mountain undulates;
The southern breeze vibrates.
Here our fraternal king
comes crooning and wandering;
In praise of him I sing.

You're wandering with pleasure
O taking rest at leisure.
O fraternal king, hear!
May you pursue the career
Of your ancestors dear!

Your territory's great
And secure is your State.
O fraternal king, hear!
May you pursue your career
As host of gods whom you revere!

For long you're Heaven-blest;
You enjoy peace and rest.
O fraternal king, hear!
May you pursue your career
And be blessed far and near!

You've supporters and aides
Virtuous of all grades
To lead or act as wing.

O our fraternal king,
Of your pattern all sing.

Majestic you appear,
Like jade-mace without peer;
You're praised from side to side.
O fraternal king, hear!
Of the State you're the guide.

The phoenixes fly
  With rustling wing
And settle high.
  Officers of the king's
Employed each one
To please the Heaven's Son.

The phoenixes fly
  With rustling wing
To azure sky.
  Officers of the king
At your command
Please people of the land.

The phoenixes sing
  On lofty height;
Planes grow in spring
  On morning bright.
Lush are plane-trees
And phoenixes sing at ease.

O many are
  Your cars and steed!
Many a steed and car
  Runs at high speed.
I sing but to prolong

Your holy song.

Note: This is the third ode addressed by Duke Kang of Zhao to King
Cheng, desiring for him long prosperity and congratulating him on the happiness of his people and the number of his admirable officers. The duke is supposed to be walking with the king on some breezy height, and entering into
the spirit of the young monarch's delight, he responds to his song with one
of his own. It is said that he who possesses all under the sky sacrifices to all
the Spirits, and thus the Son of Heaven is indeed the "host" of them all.
Stanza 5 sets forth how happiness is to be realized — by means of wise
and loyal counsellors. In stanzas 7−9, it is all imagination about such a fabulous bird as the phoenix making its appearance. It is said that the phoenix
will rest only on the plane tree, so will wise counsellors admonish only a
good king.

253. Duke Mu of Zhao's Advice

The people are hard pressed;
They need a little rest.
Do the Central Plain good,
You'll reign o'er a neighborhood.
Of the wily beware;
Against vice take care!
Put the oppressors down
Lest they fear not the crown!
Show kindness far and near;
Consolidate your sphere!

The people are hard pressed;
They need repose and rest.
Do the Central Plain good;
People will come from the neighborhood.
Of the wily beware;
Against bad men take care!
Repress those who oppress;
Relieve those in distress!

Through loyal service done
The royal quiet is won.

The people are hard pressed;
They need relief and rest.
Do good in the capital,
You'll please your people all.
Of the wily beware;
Against wicked men take care!
Repress those who oppress
Lest they go to excess!
In manner dignified
You'll have good men at your side.

The people are hard pressed;
They need some ease and rest.
Do good in Central Plain
To relieve people's pain!
Of the wily beware;
Against evil take care!
Put the oppressors down
Lest your rule be o'erthrown!
Though still young in the State,
What you can do is great.

The people are hard pressed;
They need quiet and rest.
Do good in Central Plain
Lest people suffer pain!
Of the wily beware;
Against flattery take care!
Put the oppressors down
Lest the State be o'erthrown!
O king, as jade you're nice.
Please take my frank advice!

Note: This is an ode made by Duke Mu of Zhao to reprimand King Li
(877 – 841 BC) in a time of disorder and suffering.

254. Count of Fan's Censure

God won't our kingdom bless;
People are in distress.
Your words incorrect are;
Your plans cannot reach far.
You care not what sages do;
What you say is not true.
Your plans are far from nice;
So I give you advice.

Heaven sends troubles down.
O how can you not frown?
It makes turmoil prevail;
You talk to no avail.
If what you say is right,
'Twill be heard with delight.
If what you say is not,
It will soon be forgot.

Our duties different,
We serve the government.
I give you advice good;
Your attitude is rude.
My advice is sought after;
It's no matter for laughter.
Ancient saying is good:
"Consult cutters of wood!"

Heaven is doing wrong.
How can you get along?

I'm an old lord sincere.
How can you proud appear?
I'm not proud of my age.
How can you tease a sage?
Trouble will grow like fire,
Beyond remedy when higher.

Heaven's anger displayed,
Don't cajole or upbraid!
The good and dignified
Are mute as men who died.
The people groan and sigh,
But none dare to ask why.
Wild disorder renewed,
Who'd help our multitude?

Heaven helps people mute
By whistle as by flute,
As two maces form one,
As something brought when done.
Bring anything you please,
You'll help people with ease.
They've troubles to deplore.
Don't give them any more!

Good men a fence install;
The people form a wall.
Screens are formed by each State
And each family great.
Virtue secures repose,
Walled up by kinsmen close.
Do not destroy the wall;
Be not lonely after all!

Revere great Heaven's ire

And do not play with fire!
Revere great Heaven gay
And don't drive your own way!
There's nought but Heaven knows;
It's with you where you go.
Great Heaven sees all clear;
It's with you where you appear.

Note: This censure describes the prevailing misery in the time of King Li,
complains of the want of sympathy with him shown by other officers, admonishes them and sets forth the duty required of them.

(25) Third Decade of Epics

255. Warnings

God's influence spreads vast
  Over people below.
God's terror strikes so fast;
  He deals them blow on blow.
Heaven gave people birth,
  On whom he'd not depend.
At first they're good on earth,
  But few last to the end.

"Alas!" said King Wen of the west,
  "You king of Yin-Shang, lo!
How could you have oppressed
  And exploited people so!
Why put those in high place
  Who did everything wrong?
Those who love Heaven's grace
  Are oppressed by the strong.

"Alas!" said King Wen of the west,
  "You king of Yin-Shang, lo!
Why not help the oppressed
  And give the strong a blow?
Why let rumors wide spread
  And robbers be your friend?
Let curse fall on your head
  And troubles without end!

"Alas!" said King Wen of the west,
  "You king of Yin-Shang, lo!
You do wrong without rest.

Can good out of wrong grow?
You know not what is good;
　You've no good men behind.
Good men not understood,
　To you none will be kind.

"Alas!" said King Wen of the west,
　"You king of Yin-Shang, lo!
You drink wine without rest;
　On a wrong way you go.
You know not what's about,
　Nor tell darkness from light.
Amid clamour and shout
　You turn day into night.

"Alas!" said King Wen of the west,
　"You king of Yin-Shang, lo!
Cicadas cry without rest
　As bubbling waters flow.
Things great and small go wrong
　But heedless still you stand.
Indignation grows strong
　In and out of the land.

"Alas!" said King Wen of the west,
　"You king of Yin-Shang days!
Not that you're not God-blest,
　Why don't you use old ways?
You've no experienced men,
　But the laws have come down.
Why won't you listen then?
　Your State will be o'erthrown.

"Alas!" said King Wen of the west,
　"You who wear Yin-Shang's crown!

Know what say people blest:
  When a tree's fallen down,
Its leaves may still be green
  But roots exposed to view.
Let Xia's downfall be seen
  As a warning to you!''

Note: This is a warning addressed to King Li who landed the Zhou dynasty in imminent peril by his violent oppressions, his neglect of good men, his employment of mean creatures, his reviving the old statutes and laws, his drunkenness and the fierceness of his will. The address is delivered by historical displacement, with words put into the mouth of King Wen who delivered warnings to the last king of the Shang dynasty, in the hope that King Li would transfer the figure to himself and alter his course so as to avoid a similar ruin.

256. Duke of Wei's Admonition

What appears dignified
Reveals a good inside.
You know as people say:
There're no sages but stray.
When people have done wrong,
It shows their sight's not long.
When sages make mistakes,
It shows their wisdom breaks.

If a leader is good,
He'll tame the neighborhood.
If his virtue is great,
He'll rule o'er every State.
When he gives orders,
They'll reach the borders.
As he is dignified,
He's obeyed far and wide.

Look at the present state:
Political chaos' great.
Subvert'd the virtue fine,
You are besott'd by wine.
You wish your pleasure last
And think not of the past.
Enforce the laws laid down
By kings who wore a crown!

Or Heaven won't bless you
Like water lost to view,
Till you're ruined and dead.
Rise early, late to bed!
Try to sweep the floor clean;
Let your pattern be seen!
Keep cars and steeds in rows
And your arrows and bows!
If on alert you stand,
None dare invade your land.

Do people real good;
Make laws against falsehood!
Beware of what's unforeseen;
Say rightly what you mean!
Try to be dignified;
Be kind and mild outside!
A flaw in white jade found,
Away it may be ground;
A flaw in what you say
Will leave its influence to stay.

Don't lightly say a word
Nor think it won't be heard!
Your tongue is held by none;

Your uttered words will run.
Each word will answered be;
No deed is done for free.
If you do good to friend
And people without end,
You'll have sons in a string
And people will obey you as king.

Treat your friends with good grace;
Show them a kindly face!
You should do nothing wrong
E'en when far from the throng.
Be good when you're alone;
No wrong is done but known.
Think not you are unseen;
The sight of God is keen.
You know not what is in his mind,
Let alone what's behind.

When you do what is good,
Be worthy of manhood!
With people get along;
In manners do no wrong!
Making no mistakes small,
You'll be pattern for all.
For a peach thrown on you,
Return a plum as due!
Seeking horns where there's none,
You make a childish fun.

The soft, elastic wood
For stringed lute is good.
A mild, respectful man
Will do good when he can.
If you meet a man wise,

At what you say he tries
To do what he thinks good.
But a foolish man would
Think what you say untrue:
Different is his view.

Alas! young man, how could
You tell evil from good?
I'll lead you by the hand
And show you where you stand.
I'll teach you face to face
So that you can keep pace.
I'll hold you by the ear,
You who have children dear.
If you are not content,
In vain your youth is spent.

Great Heaven fair and bright,
I live without delight.
Seeing you dream all day,
My heart will pine away.
I tell you now and again,
But I advise you in vain.
You think me useless one;
Of my words you make fun.
Can you say you don't know
How old today you grow?

Alas! young man, I pray,
Don't you know ancient ways?
Listen to my advice,
And you'll be free from vice.
If Heaven's ire comes down,
Our State would be o'erthrown.
Just take examples near by,

You'll see justice on high.
If far astray you go,
You'll plunge people in woe.

Note: This ode was made by Duke Wu of Wei at 90 not only to admonish himself but also to reprehend King Li. This was the earliest proverbial ode in Chinese poetry.

257. Misery

Lush are mulberry trees;
Their shade affords good ease.
When they're stript of their leaves,
The people deeply grieve.
They're so deeply distressed
That sorrow fills their breast.
O Heaven great and bright,
Why not pity our plight?

The steeds run far and nigh;
The falcon banners fly.
The disorder is great;
There's ruin in the State.
So many killed in clashes,
Houses reduced to ashes.
Alas! we're full of gloom;
The State is near its doom.

Nothing can change our fate;
Heaven won't help our State.
Where to stop we don't know;
We have nowhere to go.
Good men may think and brood;
They strive not for their good.

Who is the man who sows
The dire distress and woes?

With heavy heart I stand,
Thinking of my homeland.
Born at unlucky hour,
I meet God's angry power.
To the east from the west
I have nowhere to rest.
I see only disorder;
In danger is our border.

If you follow advice,
You may lessen the vice.
Let's gain a livelihood;
Put things in order good!
Who can hold something hot
If he waters it not?
Can remedy be found
If the people are drowned?

Standing against the breeze,
How can you breathe at ease?
Could people forward go
Should an adverse wind blow?
Love cultivated soil;
Let people live on toil!
The grain to them is dear;
They toil from year to year.

Heaven sends turmoil down
To ruin the royal crown.
Injurious insects reign
And devour crop and grain.
Alas! in Central State

Devastation is great.
What can I do but cry
To the boundless great sky!

If the king's good and wise,
He's revered in our eyes.
He'll make his plans with care
And choose ministers fair and square.
If he has no kinghood,
He'll think alone he's good.
His thoughts are hard to guess,
His people in distress.

Behold! among the trees
The deer may roam at ease.
Among friends insincere
You cannot roam with cheer,
No advance nor retreat
As in a strait you meet.

How wise these sages are!
Their views and words reach far.
How foolish those men bad!
They rejoice as if mad.
We can't tell them what we know
For fear of coming woe.

These good men you avoid;
They are never employed.
Those cruel men in power
Are courted from hour to hour.
So disorder is bred
And evil deeds wide spread.

The big wind blows its way

From the large, empty vale.
What can a good man say?
    It is of no avail.
In the court bad men stay;
    What they say will prevail.

The big wind blows its way;
In the court bad men stay.
When praised, they're overjoyed;
    When blamed, they play the drunk.
Good men are not employed;
    In distress they are sunk.

Alas! alas! my friend,
Can I write to no end?
Like a bird on the wing,
    Hit, you may be brought down.
Good to you I will bring,
    But at me you will frown.

Don't do wrong to excess!
People fall in distress.
If you do people wrong,
How can they get along?
If they take a wrong course,
It's because you use force.

People live in unrest,
For robbers spread like pests.
I say that will not do;
You say that is not true.
Though you think I am wrong,
I've made for you this song.

Note: The Earl of Rui mourns over the misery and disorder of the times,
with a view to reprehend the misgovernment of King Li, especially his oppres-

pressions and listening to bad counsellors. The first three lines are metaphorical of the flourishing kingdom which was now brought to the verge of ruin. In stanza 7 we have a point of time indicated clearly enough in the verse: *"Heaven sends turmoil down/ To ruin the royal crown."* This is a universal explanation of the dethronement (in effect) of King Li in 841 BC. The people then rose in revolt against him, irritated by his long-continued oppressions, and he only saved his life by flying to Shanxi, where he remained till he died in 827 BC. The ode is supposed to be composed immediately after his dethronement, and the writer regards the king as the cause of the suffering which so greatly distressed and depressed him.

258. Great Drought

The Silver River shines on high,
Revolving in the sky.
The king heaves sigh on sigh:
"Oh! what wrong have we done?
What riot has death run!
Why have famines come one by one?
What sacrifice have we not made?
Have we not burned maces of jade?
Have victims not been killed in herd?
How is it that we are not heard?

"The drought has gone to excess;
The heat has caused distress.
There's no sacrifice we've not made
For gods above we've buried jade;
In temples far and near.
There are no souls we don't revere.
The Lord of Corn can't stop the drought;
Ruin falls on our land all about.

The Almighty God won't come down.
Why should the drought fall on my crown!

"Excessive is the drought;
I am to blame, no doubt.
I palpitate with fear
As if thunder I hear.
Of people I'm bereft;
How many will be left?
The Almighty on high
Does not care if we die.
Oh! my ancestors dear,
Don't you extinction fear?

"Excessive is the drought;
No one can put it out.
The sun burns far and wide;
I have nowhere to hide.
My end is coming near;
I see no help appear.
Dukes and ministers dead
All turn away their heads.
Oh, my ancestors dear,
How can you not appear?

"The drought spreads far and nigh;
Hills are parched and streams dry.
The demon vents his ire;
He spreads wide flames and fire.
My heart's afraid of heat;
Burned with grief, it can't beat.
Why don't the souls appear?
Why don't they my prayer hear?
Almighty in the sky,
Why put on me such pressure high?

"The drought holds excessive sway,
But I dare not go away.
Why has it come from on high?
I know not the reason why.
Early I prayed for a good year,
Sacrifice offered there and here.
God in heaven, be kind!
Why won't you bear this in mind?
O my reverent Sire!
Why vent on me your ire?

"The drought has spread far and near;
People dispersed there and here.
Officials toil in vain;
The premier brings no rain.
The master of my horses
And leaders of my forces,
There's none but does his best;
There's none who takes a rest.
I look up to the sky.
What to do with soil dry?

"I look up to the sky;
The stars shine bright on high.
My officers have done their best;
With rain our land's not blessed.
Our course of life is run,
But don't give up what's done!
Pray for rain not for me
But for officials on the knee!
I look up to the sky;
Will rain and rest come from on high?"

Note: King Xuan, on the occasion of a great drought in 821 BC, expostulated
with God and all the Spirits who might be expected to succour him and his

people, asked them why they were contending with him; and detailed the measures he had taken and was still taking for the removal of the calamity. The Silver River in stanza 1 is the Chinese name for the Milky Way.

259. Count of Shen

The four mountains are high;
Their summits touch the sky.
Their spirits come on earth
To Fu and Shen gave birth.
The Shen State and Fu State
Are Zhou House's bulwarks great.
They screen it from attack
On the front and the back.

Count Shen was diligent
In royal government.
At Xie he set up capital,
A pattern for southern States all.
Count Zhao was ordered by the king
To take charge of the house-building.
Of southern States Shen's made the head,
Where his great influence will spread.

The king ordered Shen's chief
To be pattern to southern fief;
To employ men of capital
To build the city wall.
The king gave Count Zhao his command
To define Count Shen's land.
The king ordered his steward old
To remove Shen's household.

The construction of the State of Shen

Was done by Count Zhao and his men.
They built first city walls
And then the temple halls.
The great works done by the lord,
The king gave Count Shen as reward
Four noble steeds at left and right
With breasthooks amid trappings bright.

The king told Count Shen to speed
To his State in cab and steed.
"I've thought of your town beforehand;
Nowhere's better than southern land.
I confer on you this mace,
Symbol of dignity and grace.
Go, my dear uncle, go
And protect the south from the foe!"

Count Shen set out for Xie;
The king feasted him at Mei.
Count Shen would take command
At Xie in southern land.
Count Zhao was ordered to define
Shen's land and border line;
To provide him with food
That he might find his journey good.

Count Shen with flag and banner
Came to Xie, grand in manner.
His footmen and charioteers
Were greeted by the town with cheers.
The State will be guarded by men
Under the command of Count Shen,
Royal uncle people adore
And pattern in peace as in war.

Count Shen with virtue bright
Is mild, kind and upright.
He'll keep all the States in order,
With fame spread to the border.
I, Ji Fu, make this song
In praise of the count strong.
I present this beautiful air
To the count bright and fair.

Note: This epic ode celebrates the appointment by King Xuan of his uncle
to be the Count of Shen and defender of the southern border of the kingdom. The writer was General Ji Fu who appears in epic ode 177 as the
commander of an expedition against the Huns at the beginning of King
Xuan's reign.

260. Cadet Shan Fu

Heaven who made mankind
Endowed him with body and mind.
The people loved manhood.
Could they not love the good?
Heaven beheld our crown
And shed light up and down.
To help its son on earth,
To Shan Fu it gave birth.

Cadet Shan Fu is good,
Endowed with mild manhood.
Dignified is his air;
He behaves with great care.
His law is lessons old;
His strength lies where he's bold.
He follows Heaven's Son
That his orders may be done.

The king orders him to appear
As pattern to each peer;
To serve as his ancestors dear
And protect the king here;
To give orders to old and young
And be the king's throat and tongue;
To spread decrees and orders
That they be obeyed on four borders.

The orders dignified
Are spread out far and wide.
Premier Shan Fu does know
The kingdom's weal and woe.
He's wise and free from blame,
To guard his life and fame.
He's busy night and day
To serve the king for aye.

As people have said oft.
"We choose to eat the soft;
The hard will be cast out."
On this Shan Fu cast doubt.
He won't devour the soft;
Nor is the hard cast oft.
He'll do the weak no wrong,
Nor will he fear the strong.

People say everywhere,
"Virtue is light as air;
But few can bear its weight."
I often ruminate:
Its weight Shan Fu can bear;
Our love can't help him, ne'er.
When the king has defect,
Shan Fu helps him correct.

Where Shan Fu goes along,
Run his four horses strong.
His men alert would find
They often lag behind.
His four steeds run east-bound
To eight bells' tinkling sound.
The king orders him to go down
To fortify the eastern town.

His four steeds galloping,
His eight bells gaily ring.
Shan Fu goes to Qi State;
His return won't be late.
I, Ji Fu, make this song
To blow like breeze for long.
O Shan Fu, though we part,
My song will soothe your heart.

Note: This epic ode celebrates the virtue of Cadet Shan Fu, who appears to
have been the principal minister of King Xuan, and describes his mission to
the east to fortify the capital of the State of Qi. Like the preceding ode, this
was also made by General Ji Fu to present to his friend on his departure
from the court.

261. The Marquis of Han

The Liang Mountains are grand;
Yu of Xia cultivated the land.
The Marquis of Han came his way
To be invested in array.
"Serve as your fathers had done,"
In person said the Heaven's Son,
"Do not belie our trust!

Show active zeal you must!
Let things be well arranged!
Our order won't be changed.
Assist us to extort
Lords who won't come to court!"

His cab was drawn by four steeds
Long and large at high speeds.
The Marquis at court did stand,
His mace of rank in hand.
He bowed to the Heaven's Son,
Who showed him his gifts one by one.
The dragon flags all new
And screens made of bamboo,
Black robes and slippers red,
Carved hooks for horse's head,
A tiger's skin aboard
And golden rings for the lord.

The Marquis went on homeward way;
At Tu for the night he did stay.
Xian Fu invited him to dine,
Drinking a hundred vases of wine.
What were viands in the dishes?
Roast turtles and fresh fishes.
And what was the ragout?
Tender shoots of bamboo.
What were gifts furthermore?
A cab of State with horses four.
So many were the dishes fine,
The Marquis with delight did dine.

The Marquis was to wed
The king's niece in nuptial bed.
It was the daughter of Gui Fu

The Marquis came to woo.
A hundred cabs came on the way
To Gui's house in array.
Eight bells made tinkling sound,
Shedding glory around.
Virgins followed the bride in crowd
As beautiful as a cloud.
The Marquis looked around
The house in splendor drowned.

Gui Fu in war had fame.
Among the States whence he came,
He liked Han by the water,
Where he married his daughter.
In Han there are large streams
Full of tenches and breams;
The deer and doe are mild
And tigers and cats wild;
The bears or black or brown
Roam the land up and down.
His daughter Ji lived there;
She found no State more fair.

The city wall of Han
Was built by people of Yan.
Han ancestors got orders
To rule o'er tribes on borders.
The Marquis has below
Him tribes of Zhui and Mo.
He should preside as chief
Of northern States and fief;
Lay out fields, make walls strong
And dig deep moats along;
Present skins of bears brown
And fox white to the crown.

Note: This epic ode celebrates many aspects of the Marquis of Han: his investiture and King Xuan's charge to him; the gifts he received and the parting feast; his carriage; the excellence of his territory and his sway over the regions of the north.

262. Duke Hu of Zhao

Onward the rivers roared;
Forward our warriors poured.
There was no rest far and nigh;
We marched on River Huai.
Our cars drove on the way;
Our flags flew on display.
There was no peace far and nigh;
We marched on tribes of Huai.

Onward the rivers flow;
Backward our warriors go.
The State reduced to order,
We come back form the border.
There is peace east and west;
North and south there is rest.
An end is put to the strife;
The king may live a peaceful life.

On the two rivers' borders
The king gives Zhao Hu orders:
"Open up the countryside
And land and fields divide!
Let the people rule their fate
And conform to our state!
Define lands by decree
As far as Southern Sea!"

The king gives Zhao Hu orders
To inspect southern borders:
"When Wen and Wu were kings,
Your ancestors were their wings.
Say not young you appear;
Do as your fathers dear!
You have well served the State;
I'll give you favor great.

"Here is a cup of jade
And wine of millet made.
Tell your ancestors grand
I'll confer on you more land.
I'll gratify your desires
As my Sire did your Sire's."
Hu bows aground to say,
"May Heaven's Son live for aye!"

Hu bows aground again
In praise of royal reign.
He engraves Duke Zhao's song,
Wishing the king live long.
The Heaven's Son is wise;
His endless fame will rise.
His virtue is so great
That he'll rule o'er State on State.

Note: This epic ode celebrates an expedition in 825 BC against the more southern tribes of the Huai, and also the work done for King Xuan by Duke Hu of Zhao. The manner in which the king rewarded him and he responded to the royal favor is further included.

263   Expedition Against Xu

Grand and wise is the sovereign who
　　Gave charge to Minister
And Grand-Master Huang Fu,
　　Of whom Nan Zhong was ancestor.
"Put my six armies in order
　　And ready for warfare!
Set out for southern border
　　With vigilance and care!"

The king told Yin to assign
　　The task to Count Xiu Fu
To march his troops in line
　　And in vigilance too;
To go along the river shore
　　Until they reach the land of Xu;
And not to stay there any more
　　When the three tasks get through.

How dignified and grand
　　Did the Son of Heaven show!
He advanced on the land
　　Not too fast nor too slow.
The land of Xu was stirred
　　And greatly terrified
As if a thunder heard
　　Shook the land far and wide.

The king in brave array
Struck the foe with dismay.
His chariots went before;
Like tigers did men roar.
Along the riverside
They captured the foes terrified.

They advanced to the rear
And occupied their sphere.

The legions of the king's
Are swift as birds on wings.
Like rivers they are long;
Like mountains they are strong.
They roll on like the stream;
Boundless and endless they seem.
Invincible, unfathomable, great,
They've conquered the Xu State.

The king has wisely planned
How to conquer Xu's land.
Xu's chiefs come to submit
All through the king's merit.
The country pacified,
Xu's chiefs come to the king's side.
They won't again rebel,
And the king says, "All's well."

This epic ode celebrates an expedition by King Xuan against the State of
Xu, a more northern tribe of the Huai. The commander in-chief was
Huang Fu, a descendant of General Nan Zhong who had done good service
to the State against the Huns in the time of King Wen (See ode 168). (He
should be distinguished from President Huang Fu, mentioned in ode 193,
considered a very bad and dangerous man in the time of King You, King
Xuan's son and successor.)

264. Complaint Against King You

I look up to the sky;
  Great Heaven is not kind.
Restless for long am I;
  Down fall disasters blind.

Unsettled is the State;
　　We're distressed high and low.
Insects raise havoc great.
　　Where's the end to our woe?
The net of crime spreads wide.
Alas! where can we hide!

People had fields and lands,
　　But you take them away.
People had their farm hands;
　　On them your hands you lay.
This man has done no wrong;
　　You say guilty is he.
That man's guilty for long;
　　You say from guilt he's free.

A wise man builds a city wall;
A fair woman brings its downfall.
Alas! such a woman young
　　Is no better than an owl;
Such a woman with a long tongue
　　Will turn everything foul.
Disaster comes not from the sky
　　But from a woman fair.
You can't teach or rely
　　On woman and eunuch for e'er.

They slander, cheat and bluff,
　　Tell lies before and behind.
Is it not bad enough?
　　How can you love a woman unkind?
They are like men of trade
　　For whom wise men won't care.
Wise women are not made
　　For State but household affairs.

Why does Heaven's blame to you go?
　　Why won't gods bless your State?
You neglect your great foe
　　And regard me with hate.
For omens you don't care;
You've no dignified air.
Good men are not employed;
The State will be destroyed.

Heaven extends its sway
　　Over our weal and woe.
Good men have gone away;
　　My heart feels sorrow grow.
Heaven extends its sway
　　O'er good and evil deeds.
Good men have gone away;
　　My heart feels sad and bleeds.

The bubbling waters show
How deep the spring's below.
Alas! the evil sway
Begins not from today.
Why came it not before
Or after I'm no more?
Oh! boundless Heaven bright,
Nothing's beyond your might.
Bring to our fathers no disgrace
But save our future race!

Note: The writer deplores the misery and oppression that prevailed in the
time of King You (780－770 BC), and intimates that they were caused by
the interference of Lady Bao Shi in the government. In the first stanza, the
writer appeals to Heaven as if the suffering that abounded were caused by it,
and then proceeds to indicate and probe the real sources of it. The insects
from without will be Huang Fu and other bad ministers of King You, and

those from with in will be represented principally by Lady Bao Shi. By the "net of crime "we are to understand the multitude of penal laws, to whose doom people were exposed. These were never relaxed, never modified. Men were continually exposed to them; they acted as a net, which is never taken up, but is always kept in the water. Stanza 3 is specially intended for Lady Bao Shi and her creatures in the palace. In the last stanza, the manner in which the water bubbles up a spring is an evidence of its depth, and so the nature of the writer's sorrow shows that it has long been growing. The last two lines are an admonition to King You, and summon him to repentance. To this ode may be traced Chinese influence on American imagism.

265. King You's Times

Formidable Heaven on high
   Sends down big famine and disorder.
Fugitives wander far and nigh;
   Disaster spreads as far as the border.

Heaven sends down its net of crime;
   Officials fall in civil strife.
Calamitous is the hard time;
   The State can't lead a peaceful life.

Deceit and slander here and there,
   Wrong-doers win the royal grace.
Restless, cautious and full of care,
   We are afraid to lose our place.

As in a year of drought
   There can be no lush grass,
No withered leaves can sprout.
   This State will perish, alas!

We had no greater wealth
   In bygone years;

We're not in better health
  Than our former compeers.
They were like paddy fine;
  We're like coarse rice.
Why not give up your wine
  But indulge in your vice!

A pool will become dry
  When no rain falls from the skies;
A spring will become dry
  When below no waters rise.
The evil you have done will spread.
Won't it fall on my head?

In the days of Duke Zhao
  Our land ever increased.
Alas! alas! but now
  Each day our land decreased.
Men of today, behold!
Don't you know anything of old?

Note: The writer bemoans the misery and ruin which were going on, showing they were due to King You's employment of mean and worthless men.
"The writer," said a commentor in 1762, "saw that nothing now could
be done for the kingdom and that the honored capital of Zhou was near de-
struction; but in his loyal and righteous heart he could not cease to hope
concerning his sovereign. In the former ode he expresses his wish that the
king would not disgrace his great ancestors, and here that he would use
such ministers as the Duke of Zhao. A filial son will not refrain from giving
medicine to his father though he knows that his disease is incurable, and a
loyal minister will still give good advice to his sovereign though he knows
that the kingdom is on the verge of ruin." To this ode may be traced influence on *Elegies of Qu Yuan* (340 - 278 BC).

Part IV

Book of Hymns

(26) FIRST DECADE OF HYMNS OF ZHOU

266. Sacrificial Hymn to King Wen

Solemn's the temple still;
Princes their duties fulfil.
Numerous officers,
Virtuous King Wen's followers,
Worship his soul on high,
Whom they hurry to glorify.
There are none but revere
Tirelessly their ancestor dear.

Note: The hymn is a song for the music at the sacrifice in the ancestral temple. This hymn celebrates the reverential manner in which was performed a
sacrifice to King Wen (1184—1134 BC).

267. King Wen's Virtue

Great Heaven goes its way
Without cease and for aye.
Oh! King Wen's virtue great
Will likewise circulate.
His virtue overflows
And in his descendants grows.
Whate'er King Wen has done
Will profit his great-grandson.

Note: This hymn celebrates the virtue of King Wen as comparable to that of
Heaven. That is the reason why his successors were called Sons of Heaven.

268. King Wen's Statutes

The world is clear and bright;
King Wen's statutes shed light.
They begin by sacrificial rite
And end by victory great.
God, bless Zhou's State!

Note: It is said that this hymn was sung at the end of the sacrifice and
hymn 266 at its beginning.

269. King Cheng's Address in 1109 BC

O princes bright and brave,
Favored by former kings!
Boundless blessings we have
Will pass to our offsprings.
Don't sin against your State!
You will be honored as before.
Think of your service great,
And you'll enlarge it more.
If you employ wise men,
All States will feel your influence then.
If you're virtuous in all things,
Your example affords
A pattern for all lords.
Ah! Don't forget our former kings!

Note: This piece was made on the occasion of King Cheng's accession to
the government in 1109 BC, when he thus addressed the princes who had assisted him in the ancestral temple.

270. Mount Qi

Heaven made lofty hill
For former kings to till.
King Tai worked the land
For King Wen to expand.
The former kings are gone;
The mountain path is good to travel on.
Oh! ye son and grandson,
Pursue what your forefathers have begun!

Note: This hymn was appropriate to a sacrifice to King Tai who worked the land at the foot of Mount Qi (See epic 241).

271. King Cheng's Hymn

By great Heaven's decrees
·Two kings with power were blest.
King Cheng dared not live at ease
  But night and day did his best
  To rule the State without rest
  And pacify east and west.

Note: This hymn was appropriate to a sacrifice to King Cheng (reigned 1109 – 1076 BC), son of King Wu and grandson of King Wen.

272. King Wu's Sacrificial Hymn

I offer sacrifice
Of ram and bull so nice.
May Heaven bless my State!
I observe King Wen's statutes great;
I'll pacify the land.
O King Wen grand!

Come down and eat, I pray!
Do I not night and day
Revere Almighty Heaven?
May your favor to me be given!

Note: This hymn was appropriate to a sacrifice to King Wen in the audience
hall where King Wu assembled all the princes to undertake an expedition
against the last king of Shang in 1121 BC.

273. King Wu's Tour

A progress through the States is done.
O Heaven, bless your son!
    O bless the Zhou House up and down!
Our victory is so great
That it shakes State on State.
We revere gods for ever
Of mountain and of river.
    Our king is worthy of the crown.
Zhou's house is bright and full of grace;
Each lord is in his proper place,
With spears and shields stored up in rows,
And in their cases arrows and bows.
The king will do his best
To rule the kingdom east and west.
    O may our king be blest!

Note: This hymn was appropriate to King Wu's sacrifice to Heaven and to
the Spirits of the mountains and rivers on a inspection tour of the kingdom
after the overthrow of the Shang dynasty in 1121 BC.

274. Kings Cheng and Kang

King Wu was full of might;
He built a career bright.
God gives Cheng and Kang charge
This glory to enlarge.
Kings Cheng and Kang are blest
To rule from east to west.
How splendid is their reign!
Hear drums' and bells' refrain!
Hear stones and flutes resound!
With blessings we are crowned.
Blessings come to our side;
Our lords look dignified.
We are drunk and well fed;
Blessings come on our head.

Note: This hymn was appropriate to a sacrifice to King Wu and Kings
Cheng and Kang, his son and grandson.

275. To Hou Ji, Lord of Corn

O Lord of Grain and Corn so bright,
You're at God's left or right.
You gave people grain-food;
None could do us more good.
God makes us live and eat;
You told us to plant wheat.
We don't define our border
But we live in good order.

Note: This hymn was appropriate to the border sacrifice when Hou Ji, the
Lord of Corn and Grain, was worshipped as the correlate of God. (See
epic 245)

(27) SECOND DECADE OF HYMNS OF ZHOU

276. Husbandry

Ah! ye ministers dear,
Attend to duties here!
The king's set down the rule
You should know to the full.
Ah! ye officers dear,
It is now late spring here.
What do you seek to do?
Tend the fields old and new!
Wheat grows lush in the field.
What an enormous yield!
Ah! Heaven bright and clear
Will give us a good year.
Men, get ready to wield
Your sickles, spuds and hoes
And reap harvest in rows!

Note: This is the first hymn of Zhou dealing with husbandry. These were instructions given to the officers of husbandry, probably after the spring sacrifice for a good year.

277. King Kang's Prayer

O King Cheng in the sky,
Please come down from on high!
See us lead the campaign
To sow all kinds of grain,
And till our fields with glee
All over thirty li!

Ten thousand men in pairs
Plough the land with the shares.

Note: This is a hymn sung by King Kang after the sacrifice to his father,
King Cheng, for a good year.

278. Guest Assisting at Sacrifice

Rows of egrets in flight
O'er the marsh in the west.
Like those birds dressed in white,
Here comes our noble guest.
He's loved in his own State;
He is welcome in ours.
Be it early or late,
His fame for ever towers.

Note: This hymn celebrates the representative of the former dynasty who
had come to court to assist at sacrifice. The egret was prized for the pure
white of its plumage, and its movements were also supposed to be remarkable for their elegance. Here the deportment of the visitor is supposed to be
as elegant as the movements of the bird.

279. Thanksgiving

Millet and rice abound this year;
High granaries stand far and near.
There are millions of measures fine;
We make from them spirits and wine
And offer them to ancestors dear.
Then we perform all kinds of rites
And call down blessings from Heaven bright.

Note: This hymn of thanksgiving for a plentiful year was used at the sacrifice
in autumn and winter.

280. Temple Music

Musicians blind, musicians blind,
Come to the temple court behind!
The plume-adorned posts stand
With teeth-like frames used by the band;
From them suspend drums large and small
And sounding stones withal.
Music is played when all's complete;
We hear pan-pipe, flute and drumbeat.
What sacred melody
And solemn harmony!
Dear ancestors, give ear;
Dear visitors, come here!
You will enjoy our song
And wish it to last long.

Note: This hymn was made on the occasion of the Duke of Zhou's
completing his instruments of music and announcing the news in a grand per-
formance in the temple of King Wen.

281. Sacrifice of Fish

In Rivers Ju and Qi
Fish in warrens we see.
There're sturgeons large and small,
Mudfish, carp we enthral
For temple sacrifice
That we may be blessed twice.

Note: This hymn was sung in the month of winter and in spring when the king presented a fish in the ancestral temple as an act of duty and an acknowledgement that it was to his ancestors' favor that the king and the people were indebted for the supplies of food which they received from the waters.

282. King Wu's Prayer to King Wen

We come in harmony;
We stop in gravity,
The princes at the side
Of the king dignified.

"I present this bull nice
And set forth sacrifice
To royal father great.
Bless your filial son and his State!

"You're a sage we adore,
A king in peace and war.
O give prosperity
To Heaven and posterity!

"Bless me with a life long,
With a State rich and strong!
I pray to father I revere
And to my mother dear."

Note: This hymn was appropriate at a sacrifice by King Wu to his father Wen. In Confucius' time the three great families of the State of Lu used this piece in sacrificing in their ancestral temples, to the great dissatisfaction of the sage.

283. King Cheng at King Wu's Temple

The lords appear before the king
  To learn the rules he ordains.
    The dragon flags are bright
And the carriage bells ring.
  Glitter the golden reins,
    His splendor at its height.
The filial king leads the throng
  Before his father's shrine.
He prays to be granted life long
  And to maintain his rights divine.
May Heaven bless his State!
  The princes brave and bright
Be given favors great
  That they may serve at left and right.

Note: This hymn was appropriate to an occasion when the feudal princes
were assisting King Cheng at a sacrifice to his father Wu in 1113 BC.

284. Guests at the Sacrifice

Our guests alight
From horses white.
Their train is long,
A noble throng.

Stay here one night
Or two or four!
Fasten their horses tight
Lest they should leave the door!

Escort them on their way;
Say left and right, "Good day!"

Say "Good day" left and right
Till day turns into night.

Note: This piece celebrates the Viscount Wei on one of his appearances at
the capital and assisting at the sacrifice in the ancestral temple of Zhou. It
shows how he was esteemed and cherished by the king as an uncle of the
last king of the Shang dynasty. When the rebellion of the last king's son
was put down and the son himself put to death, the Viscount Wei was made
duke of Song so that he might continue the sacrifice of the House of Shang.

285. Hymn to King Wu

O King Wu great and bright,
Matchless in main and might.
King Wen beyond compare
Opened the way for his heir.
King Wu after his sire
Quelled Yin's tyrannic fire.
His fame grows higher and higher.

Note: This hymn was sung in the ancestral temple to the music regulating
the dance in honor of the achievements of King Wu. Perhaps it was only a
prelude to the dance.

(28) THIRD DECADE OF HYMNS OF ZHOU

286. Elegy on King Wu

Alas! how sad am I!
O'er my deceased father I cry.
Lonely, I'm in distress
To lose my father whom gods bless.
Filial all your life long,
You loved grandfather strong
As if he were e'er in courtyard.
Fatherless, I am thinking hard
Of you both night and day.
O kings to be remembered for aye!

Note: This elegy was made by King Cheng on his repairing to the temple
when the mourning for his father Wu was expired.

287. King Cheng's Coronation

I seek, when begins my sway,
To follow my father's way.
Ah! but he's far above me;
To reach him I am not free.
However hard I have tried,
I cannot get to his side.
I'm a young king not so great
To shoulder hard tasks of the State.
I look for him up and down;
How to attain his renown?
O my royal father dear,
Help me to be bright and clear!

Note: This seems to be a sequel to the former hymn. The young king tells of his difficulties and incompetences, asks for counsel to help to copy the example of his father Wu, and concludes with an appeal or prayer to his father.

288. King Cheng and His Ministers

"Be reverent, be reverent!
The way of Heaven's evident.
Do not let its favor pass by
Nor say Heaven's remote on high!
It rules over our rise and fall
And daily watches over all."
"I am a young king of our State,
But I will show reverence great.
As sun and moon shine day and night,
I will learn to be fair and bright.
Assist me to fulfil my duty
And show me high virtue and beauty!"

Note: This piece may be a portion of the consultation which took place in the temple between King Cheng and his ministers. In the first six lines we have the admonitions of the ministers and in the remaining six the reply of the king.

289. King Cheng's Self-Criticism

I blame myself for woes gone by
And guard against those of future nigh.
A wasp is a dangerous thing.
Why should I seek its painful sting?
At first only a wren is heard;
When it takes wing, it becomes a bird.
Unequal to hard tasks of the State

I am again in a narrow strait.

Note: King Cheng acknowledges that he has erred and states his intention
to be careful in the future; he will guard against the slight beginnings of evil
and is overcome with a sense of his own incompetence. This piece may be
considered to be the conclusion of the service in the ancestral temple with
which it and the previous three are connected.

290. Cultivation of the Ground

The grass and bushes cleared away,
The ground is ploughed at break of day.
A thousand pairs weed hoe in hand;
They toil in old or new-tilled land.

The master comes with all his sons,
The older and the younger ones.
They are all strong and stout;
At noon they take meals out.
They love their women fair,
Who take of them good care.

With the sharp plough they wield,
They break the southern field.
All kinds of grain they sow
Burst into life and grow.
Young shoots without end rise,
The longest strike the eyes.
The grain grows lush here and there;
The toilers weed with care.

The reapers come around;
The grain's piled up aground.
There're millions of stacks fine
To be made food or wine.

For our ancestors' shrine
And for the rites divine.

The delicious food
Is glory of kinghood.
The fragrant wine, behold!
Gives comfort to the old.

We reap not only here,
    Nor only for today.
From olden days we've reapt with cheer;
    We reap just in our fathers' way.

Note: This piece was an accompaniment to some royal sacrifice. It brings before us a series of pleasing pictures of the husbandry of the early times.

291. Thanksgiving in Autumn

Sharp are the plough-shares we wield;
We plough the southern field.
All kinds of grain we sow
Burst into life and grow.

Our wives come to the ground
With baskets square and round
Of millet and steamed bread,
With straw-hat on their heads.

We weed with hoe in hand
On the dry or wet land.
When weeds fall in decay,
Luxuriant millets sway.

When millets rustling fall,

We reap and pile them up all
High and thick as a wall.
Like comb teeth stacks are close;
Stores are opened in rows.
Wives and children repose
When all of them are full.

We kill a tawny bull,
Whose horns crooked appear.
We follow fathers dear
To perform rites with cheer.

Note: This hymn was made to thank the Spirits of the land and the grain in autumn and therefore it sets forth the beginning and the end of labors of husbandry.

292. Supplementary Sacrifice

In silken robes clean and bright,
In temple caps for the rite,
The officers come from the hall
To inspect tripods large and small,
To see the sheep and oxen down and up,
And rhino horns used as cups,
To see if mild is wine,
If there is noise before the shrine
In sacrifice to lords divine.

Note: This piece was appropriate to a sacrifice and the feast after it. It belonged to the entertainment of the personators of the dead in connection with the supplementary sacrifice on the day after one of the great sacrifices in the ancestral temple.

293. The Martial King

The royal army brave and bright
  Was led by King Wu in dark days
To o'erthrow Shang and bring back light
  And establish the Zhou House's sway.
Favored by Heaven, I
  Succeed the Martial King.
I'll follow him as nigh
  As summer follows spring.

Note: This was King Cheng's hymn in praise of King Wu, the Martial King, who reigned 1121 – 1115 BC. It was composed to accompany a dance performed in the temple of King Wu, the completion of which represents the achievements of the king in the overthrow of the Shang and the establishment of the Zhou dynasty. Hymn 285 and the three that follow this hymn were also sung in connection with that dance.

294. Hymn to King Wu

All the States pacified,
Heaven favors Zhou far and wide.
Rich harvest from year to year.
How mighty King Wu did appear
With his warriors and cavaliers
Guarding his four frontiers
And securing his Start!
Favored by Heaven great,
Zhou replaced Shang by fate.

Note: This hymn is considered to have been a portion of a larger piece which was sung in accompaniment to the dance celebrating the merit and success of King Wu.

295. King Wu's Hymn to King Wen

King Wen's career is done;
I'd follow him as son,
Think of him without cease
And conquer Shang to seek peace.
It is Heaven's decree
To be done in high glee.

This hymn praising King Wen is said to have been the third of the pieces sung to the dance mentioned in the note on hymn 293.

296. King Wu's Progress

Oh! great is the Zhou State!
  I climb up mountains high
To see hills undulate
  And two rivers flow by.
  All under boundless sky
Come within sight; I see
It is Heaven's decree.

Note: This hymn is said to have been the fourth of the six pieces sung to the dance celebrating the greatness of Zhou and its firm possession of the kingdom, as seen in King Wu's progress.

(29) HYMNS OF LU

297. Horses

How sleek and large the horses are
Upon the plain of borders far!
What color are these horses bright?
Some black and white, some yellow light.
Some are pure black, others are bay.
What splendid chariot steeds are they!
The Duke of Lu has clear fore-sight:
He has prepared his steeds to fight.

How sleek and large the horses are
Upon the plain of borders far!
What color are these horses bright?
Some piebald, others green and white.
Some brownish red, some dapple grey.
What fiery chariot steeds are they!
The Duke of Lu has good fore-sight:
He will employ his steeds in fight.

How sleek and large the horses are
Upon the plain of borders far!
What color are these steeds well-trained?
Some flecked; some white and black-maned;
Some black and white-maned; others red.
They are chariot horses well-bred.
The Duke of Lu has fine fore-sight:
He's bred and trained his steeds to fight.

How sleek and large the horses are
Upon the plain of borders far!
What color are these horses bright?

Some cream-like, others red and white;
some white-legged, some fishlike-eyed.
They drive war chariots side by side.
The Duke of Lu has grand fore-sight:
He will drive his brave steeds to fight.

Note: King Cheng, because of the great services rendered to the kingdom by
the Duke of Zhou, granted to his eldest son, the first Marquis of Lu, the
privilege of using the royal ceremonies and music, in consequence of which
Lu had its hymns. This hymn celebrates Duke Xi of Lu (658–626 BC) for
his constant and admirable thoughtfulness, especially as seen in the number
and quality of his horses.

298. The Ducal Feast

Sleek and strong, sleek and strong,
Four brown steeds come along.
The officers are wise,
Stay late but early rise.
Like egrets white
Dancers alight.
The drums resound;
Tipsy, they dance aground;
In happiness they're drowned.

sleek and strong, sleek and strong,
Four stallions come along.
The officers drink wine;
Early and late they're fine.
Like egrets white
Dancers in flight.
The drums resound;
Drunk, they go round.
In happiness they're drowned.

Sleek and strong, sleek and strong,
four grey steeds come along.
The officers eat food;
Early and late they're good.
From now and here,
Abundant be each year!
The duke's well done,
So will his son and grandson.
They will be happy everyone.

Note: This hymn relates how Duke Xi of Lu feasted his officers and how the officers expressed their good wishes.

299. The Marquis of Lu

Pleasant is the pool half round
Where plants of cress abound.
The Marquis of Lu comes nigh;
His dragon banners fly,
His flags wave on the wing
And his carriage bells ring.
Officers old and young
Follow him all along.

Pleasant is the pool half round
Where water-weeds abound.
The Marquis of Lu comes near;
His horses grand appear.
His horses appear strong;
His carriage bells ring long.
With smiles and with looks bland,
He'll instruct and command.

Pleasant is the pool half round

Where mallow plants abound.
The Marquis pays a call
And drinks wine in the hall.
After wine, it's foretold,
You will never grow old.
If along the way you go,
You will overcome the foe.

The Marquis' virtue high
Is well-known far and nigh.
His manner dignified,
He's ever people's guide.
He's bright as well as brave,
Worthy son of ancestors grave.
He's full of filial love
And seeks blessings from above.

The Marquis of Lu bright
Sheds his virtuous light.
He's built the poolside hall;
Huai tribes pay him homage all.
His tiger-like compeers
Present the foe's left ears.
His judges wisdom show;
They bring the captive foe.

His officers aligned
With their forces combined
Drove in martial array
Southeastern tribes away.
They came on backward way
Without noise or display.
At poolside hall they show
What they've done with the foe.

They notch their arrows long
On bows with bone made strong.
Their chariots show no fears,
With tireless charioteers.
The tribes of Huai they quell
Dare no longer rebel.
As the Marquis would have it,
The tribes of Huai submit.

The owls flying at ease
Settle on poolside trees.
They eat our mulberries
And sing sweet melodies.
The chief of Huai tribes brings
All rare and precious things:
Ivory tusks, tortoise old,
Southern metals and gold.

Note: This is a hymn in praise of Marquis or Duke Xi of Lu, celebrating his
interest in the State college built by the poolside and his triumph over the
tribes of the Huai, which was celebrated in the poolside hall by presenting
the prisoners and the left ears of the slain cut off by his soldiers.

300. Hymn to Marquis of Lu

Solemn the temple stand,
Well-built, well-furnished, grand.
There we find Jiang Yuan's shrine:
Her virtue was divine.
On God she did depend
And safely by the end
Of her ten months was born
Hou Ji, our Lord of Grain and Corn.
Blessed by Heaven, he knew
When sowing time was due

For wheat and millet early or late.
Invested with a State,
He taught people to sow
The millet and to grow
The sorghum and the rice.
All o'er the country nice
He followed Yu of Xia's advice.

The grandson of Hou Ji,
    King Tai came to install
Himself south of Mount Qi,
    Nearer to Shang capital.
Then came Kings Wen and Wu;
    They both followed King Tai.
King Wu beat Shang in Mu,
    Decreed by Heaven high.
"You'd have no fear nor doubt
    For great God is with you.
You'll wipe Shang forces out,
    With victory in view."
King Cheng said to his uncle great,
    "I'll set up your eldest son
As marquis of Lu State
    And enlarge the land you've won
To protect the Zhou State."

The Duke of Lu was made
Marquis in the east obeyed,
And given land to cultivate,
Hills, rivers and attached State.
He was Duke of Zhou's grandson
And Duke Zhuang's eldest son.
With dragon banners at command,
He came six reins in hand.
He made his offering

In autumn as in spring
To God in Heaven great
And Hou Ji of Zhou State.
He offered victims nice
For the great sacrifice
And received blessings twice
From his ancestors dear;
E' en the Duke of Zhou did appear.

In summer came the rite;
   In autumn horns were capped of bull.
There were bulls red and white,
   Bull-figured goblets full,
Roast pig, soup and minced meat,
   And dishes of bamboo and wood,
And dancers all complete
   Blessed be ye grandsons good!
May you live in prosperity
   And protect the eastern land!
May you have longevity
   And may the land of Lu long stand!
Unwaning moon, unsunken sun,
   No flocd nor earthquake far and nigh.
In long life you' re second to none,
   And firm as mountains high.

A thousand cars of war were seen;
   Each had two spears with tassels red
And two bows bound by bands green.
   Thirty thousand men the duke led
In shell-adorned helmets were drest.
   They marched in numbers great
To quell the tribes of north and west
   And punish southern State.
None of them could stand your attack.

May you enjoy prosperity!
With hoary hair and wrinkled back,
    May you enjoy longevity!
Age will give you advice.
    May you live great and prosperous
To a thousand years old or twice!
    May you live long and vigorous
As eyebrows long unharmed by vice!

Lofty is the Mountain Tai
    Looked up to from Lu State.
Mounts Gui and Meng stand nigh
    And eastward undulate
As far as eastern sea.
    Huai tribes make no ado
But go down on their knee
    Before the Marquis of Lu.

We have Mounts Fu and Yi
    And till at Xu the ground
Which extends to the sea
    Where barbarians are found.
No southern tribe dare disobey
    The Marquis of Lu's command;
None but would homage pay
    To the Marquis in his land.

Heaven gives Marquis blessings great
    And a long life to rule o'er Lu.
He shall restore Duke of Zhou's State
    And dwell at Chang and Xu.
The Marquis feasts his ministers
    With his fair wife and mother old
And other officers
    For the State he shall hold.

He shall be blessed with golden hairs
And juvenile teeth like his heir's.

The hillside cypress and pine
   Are cut down from the root;
Some as long as eight feet or nine,
   Some as short as one foot.
They are used to build temples new
   With inner chambers large and long.
Behold! the temples stand in view.
   It is Xi Si who makes this song
Which reads so pleasant to the ear
That people will greet him with cheer.

Note: This is the longest epic ode or hymn in praise of Marquis or Duke Xi of Lu, celebrating his magnificent career which would make the State of Lu all that it had ever been. It was written by Xi Si on an occasion when the Marquis had repaired on a grand scale the temple of the State. It was condemned that the princes of Lu should be privileged to employ royal ceremonies and sacrifices, but it was not for the writer to call into question the legality of celebrations in which he took part and which he considered to reflect the glory of the State. He was evidently in a poetic rapture as to what his ruler was and would do.

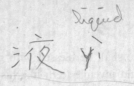

301. Sacrificial Hymn to King Tang

How splendid! how complete!
   Let's put the drums in place.
Listen to their loud beat,
   Ancestor of our race!

Your descendants invite
Your spirit to alight
By resounding drumbeat
And by flute's music sweet.
In harmony with them
Chimes the sonorous gem.

The descendants with cheer
   Listen to music bright.
Bells and drums fill the ear,
   And dancers seem in flight;
Our visitors appear
   Also full of delight.

Our sires since olden days
Showed us the proper ways
To be meek and polite
And mild from morn to night.
May you accept the rite
Your filial grandson pays!

Note: This hymn was appropriate to a sacrifice to King Tang the Successful, who overthrew the dynasty of Xia and founded that of Shang in 1765 BC. It dwells especially on music and on the reverence with which the service was performed.

302. Hymn to King Tang

Ah! ah! ancestor dear,
Shower down blessings here!
Let your blessings descend
On your sons without end!

Our wine is clear and sweet.
Make our happiness complete!
Our soup is tempered well,
Good in flavor and smell.

We pray but silently;
Bless us with longevity,
White hair and wrinkled brow!
We have no contention now.

In cars with wheels leather-bound,
At eight bells' tinkling sound,
The princes come to pray
That we'd be blessed for aye.

O give us far and near
Rich harvest year by year!
O ancestor, alight!
May you accept the rite
Your filial grandsons pay
And bless us as we pray!

Note: This hymn focuses on the spirits, the soup, the gravity of the service
and the assisting princes.

303. Hymn to Kings Tang and Wu Ding

Heaven sent a Swallow down
　　To give birth to the Sire
Of Shang who wore the crown
　　Of land of Yin entire.

God ordered Marshal Tang
　　To conquer four frontiers,
To appoint lords of Shang
　　To rule o'er the nine spheres.

The forefathers of Shang
　　Reigned by Heaven's decree.
King Wu Ding, descendant of Tang,
　　Now rules o'er land and sea.

Wu Ding's a martial king,
　　Victor second to none.
Ten dragon chariots bring
　　Sacrifice on the run.

His land extends a thousand lis
　　Where people live and rest.
He reigns as far as the four seas.
　　Lords come from east and west.

They gather at the capital
　　To pay homage in numbers great.
O good Heaven, bless all
　　The kings of the Yin State!

Note: The Sire of Shang was said to be born around 2300 BC when his mother bathing in some open place took and swallowed an egg dropped by a swallow. Marshal Tang founded the dynasty and his grandson moved the capital to Yin. This hymn was specially intended to honor King Wu Ding (1328 – 1263 BC).

304. Rise of the House of Shang

The Sire of Shang was wise;
　Good omens had appeared for long.
Seeing the deluge rise,
　He helped Yu stem the current strong,
Extend the State's frontier
　And domain far and wide.
He was son born from Swallow queer
　And Princess of Song, its bride.

He held successful sway
　Over States large and small.
He followed his proper way
　To inspect all and instruct all.
Xiang Tu, his martial grandson,
　Ruled over land and sea he had won.

Heaven's favor divine
　Lasted down to the martial King.
Toward his lords benign,
　In praise of God he'd often sing.
His virtue grows day by day;
　It is God he reveres.
God orders him to hold sway
　And be model to the nine spheres.

He received ensigns large and small
From subordinate princes all.
He received blessings from on high
For which he did not seek nor vie.
To lords he was not hard or soft;
His royal rule was gentle oft.
He received favors from aloft.

He received tributes small and large
Subordinate States did discharge.
He received favors from on high;
He showed his valor far and nigh.
Unshaken, he was fortified,
Unscared, unterrified.
All blessings came to his side.

His banners flying higher,
   His battle-ax in his fist,
The Martial King came like fire
   Whom no foe could resist.
Xie Jie was like the roots
   Which could no longer grow
When he lost his three shoots,
   Wei, Gu, Kun Wu, Tang's former foe.
   So the martial King ruled high and low.

In times when ruled King Tang,
There was prosperity for Shang.
Heaven favored his son
With Premier Ah Heng to run
The government and the State
At left and right of the prince great.

Note: This epic ode or hymn celebrates four figures: Qi the Sire of Shang who helped Yu of Xia stem the deluge around 2200 BC; Xiang Tu his grandson; Tang the martial King who founded the Shang dynasty; and Yi Yin or Ah Heng, Tang's chief advisor, on the occasion of a great sacrifice when all the previous kings of the dynasty and the lords of Shang and their famous ministers and advisors were honored in the service, probably in the year 1713 BC.

305. Hymn to King Wu Ding

How rapid did Yin troops appear!
They attacked Chu State without fear.
They penetrated into its rear
And brought back many a captive's ear.
Wu Ding conquered the Chu lands.
What an achievement grand!

The king gave Chu command,
"South of our State you stand.
In the time of King Tang
Even the tribes of Jiang
Dared not but come to pay
Homage under his sway.
Such was the rule of Shang."

Heaven gave lords its orders
To build their capitals within Yu's borders,
To pay homage each year,
To do their duties, not to fear
Its punishment severe
If farmwork's well done far and near.

Heaven ordered the lords to know
The reverent people below.
They'd do no wrong nor be
Indolent and carefree.
To each subordinate State
May be brought blessings great!

The capital was full of order,
A model for States on the border.

The king had great renown
And brilliance up and down
He enjoyed longevity.
May he bless his posterity!

We climbed the mountain high
Where pine and cypress   pierced the sky.
We felled them to the ground
And hewed them square and round.
We built with beams of pine
And pillars large and fine
The temple for Wu Ding's shrine.

Note: This hymn celebrates both the success of the war waged by King Wu Ding against the southern tribe of Chu, and the general happiness and virtue of his reign. It was probably made when a special temple was built in 1256 BC.